Celestial Song Of Creation

Annalee Skarin

CONTENTS

FOREWORD

Here is a record of glory, revealing the method of achieving the heights, the way to unfold understanding of the Almighty Truths of God.

If you would awaken your soul to the divine symphony of the Universe, follow the way of "overcoming," the Way Christ trod. The record of His Path, the eternal, inner truths of power and fulfillment are now open, the sacred, inner knowledge that has lain dormant and in the depths of your being.

Ludwig Van Beethoven, who had become deaf, humbly acknowledged that his Symphony No. 9 came to him directly from God, and that he merely transcribed it.

What is man's soul? It is his true being, where God has placed a seed of Himself, and this seed contains the perfect pattern for man's individual destiny. The soul holds all the answers to one's outside problems and inner questioning. It is the source of all inspiration and contains the power of all achievement and happiness. The soul is the innermost being of man himself.

To contact the soul, one learns "to be still!" This divine search fulfills man's conquest of himself as he begins to live God's laws. As one learns "to love God with all his heart, all his soul, all his mind, and all his strength," he begins to find the joy and the meaning of existence. The search is one that no man can make for another. It is a quest which each individual must undertake for himself. It is each individual's own responsibility.

PREFACE

The other books preceding this one were written to prepare the way for this Celestial Song of Creation. This record of glory reveals the method of exalting, triumphant achievement as it reaffirms the truths established within the souls of men.

When one's spirit is alert and his mind is searching for truth he will hear within the words and phrases and thoughts contained in this work the divine Symphony of the Universe. And that symphony will awaken his own soul to rise up and fulfill its own dynamic destiny. It will whisper its secrets of celestial glory into the fibres and tissues of the adoring heart. Then increasing in crescendo it will expand the individual's understanding to comprehend the ever-lasting Truths of Almighty God and the unspeakable powers thereof as they are fulfilled in man. These divine powers and graces are man's to use at all times.

This record, which God has so tenderly placed in your hands, reveals the way of "overcoming"—the Way Christ trod. And this Way becomes your own.

Never since time began has the challenge for man to seek to know his own soul been so great, nor has his opportunities been so close at hand. Not since Christ's advent on this earth, has the time for spiritual progress been so propitious.

"Oh man of a million mystic, unfathomed, subtle and unused powers which have lain dormant within, leave your mortal thinking habits and negatious restrictions behind and step forth into the full measure of your creation."

THE ARCHIVES OF THE SOUL

Chapter I

The other books that have been released have been sent forth to feed and enlighten the hearts and minds of men. This record is written for the awakening of your souls. This is the record that must reach beyond thought into those forgotten memories that have remained unrecalled throughout your mortal lives. This work is to reveal the ancient knowledge that has been silenced for ages by the outward strivings of man's physical nature.

This work contains the "secret, inner doctrine," known of old. It contains the sacred, inner knowledge which has lain dormant and unremembered in the innermost depths of your own beings.

Therefore, *it is given to abide in you*: the record of heaven; the Comforter; the peaceable things of immortal glory; the truth of all things; that which quickeneth all things, which maketh alive all things; that which knoweth all things, and hath all power, according to wisdom, mercy, truth, justice and judgment." (Moses 6:61 from the Pearl of Great Price).

It is to open these archives of knowledge and re-establish the eternal, inner truths of power and fulfillment that this record has been permitted to come into your hands. This record is sacred. Guard it well.

All who so desire may now begin to travel the sacred,

inner way of Life and Truth—"The Straight and Narrow Way." As you throw off the bondage of mortal thinking you will begin to travel a highway of immortality. Such a journey is only for the strong. Those who continually look backward are unfit for the kingdom. Each backward glance is retrogressive. All backwardness is unproductive and re-creates the vibrations and the conditions of the past but with even less light than before. One's errors and mistakes, if unrelinquished, only retard one's progress. Mortal think-ing with all its sordid, mortal memories must be left be-hind—after they are repented of. And repentance is the "overcoming" of the weaknesses or habit or tendency that caused the sin.

As one determinedly focuses his eyes upon his divine goal and holds his "eyes single to the glory of God" he will soon become aware that the road he travels is the transparent, gold-paved street of unimaginable beauty. He will realize also that the purified gold has been created and established by the righteousness of the flame-shod feet of advancing man.

So it is to your soul that I now speak for it is your soul that must become awake and aware of "EXISTENCE," which means literally to "STAND FORTH!"

It is your own individual soul that must now make this journey. It is your most holy, divine, beautiful, shining soul alone that has the power to tread so sacred a path.

As you go forth along this "Straight and Narrow Way" you will have the power to take your body with you for it will become purified in the journey for this is the way of purification. As you knowingly and with full awareness, travel this highway of Light, that glorifying Light is in-creased and established in all its power right within you.

This is redemption. This is the method by which one obtains release from all mortal shackles and physical bondage and soul captivity without the need to lay his body down. In this sacred journey the body becomes purified and exalted to the status of the Spirit in which condition only, can one receive a fulness of joy, which has been promised.

The noble and great ones who travel this way have no need for the inferior gift of "salvation" for they will not require the difficult, often humiliating, painful experience of being "salvaged." Salvation means to be salvaged and it is not a glamorous word nor is it a position to set as one's goal. "Salvation" is for sinners who do not overcome in this life. These are the ones who have made no attempt to believe His gentle command: "Be ye perfect, even as your Father in Heaven is perfect." And because they have not believed they have not even attempted to fulfill. To fulfill this commandment requires the great out-pouring, forgiving love that brings its own forgiveness and power of overcoming.

The great ones, having "overcome" will be exalted. To them the great front door, by-passing death, will be opened wide. These noble ones enter the higher realms as feasted sons of glory. They completely by-pass that dreary, back-door entrance, death—the servants' entrance. These are the ones who triumph over mortality. These are they who enter the higher realms exalted and glorified.

God be praised for a day so great and for such noble, divine ones as you!

Welcome! A thousand times welcome along the road of overcoming! And as you come, lift your heads high in songs of everlasting praise! Open your ears to hear and you will have the power to hear the heavenly hosts join in that singing, glorious cry of wondrous, welcoming triumph!

These are not new truths I am revealing. These are the eternal truths contained in that "sacred, inner doctrine." These are the breathtaking truths of God that your souls have always known—and unconsciously longed for. Rejoice! For now, at last, you are to be reminded of the ancient promises given to you before the world was.

The way is yours. It always has been but you have not been aware of it because of the hardness of your hearts and because of the "traditions of the fathers," which traditions came about by man's rejection of truth as each sought only for the self-satisfaction of his own mortal desires. And the darkness grew and expanded until "darkness has covered the earth and gross darkness the minds of the people." The veil of ignorance and unbelief and consequent distress has become almost impregnable. And the blindness of men's minds and the hardness of their hearts has completed the shackling hold of darkness. This world cannot sink any lower into sin and suffering and wilful wickedness without being completely destroyed. For this reason and for the sake of the righteous, these truths have come forth through the command of God. The time is NOW!

Out of man's thoughts and actions and his retaliating, discordant re-actions has that veil been woven. And it is man who will have to rend that dismal veil of darkness as he steps forth determinedly into the Light.

As you great and noble ones lift your heads and open up your hearts, through love, and your minds to be-lieve, or to BE and LIVE the higher laws, you will begin to comprehend all truth and be given all power.

Those who have not been able to comprehend, or those

who have not even desired to fulfill the truths given forth to enlighten the minds and the hearts, will have no power to touch or to understand this record. To such the great truths, engraved upon the very fibres of their own souls, will continue to remain uncomprehended and unfulfilled.

But you who can read, read! And you who can understand, give ear! This record is already engraved within the recesses of your own divine, innermost beings! "For it is given to abide in you, the record of heaven!"

Come! Leave the darkness behind! Leave the old, worn-out, desolating habits of mortal thinking and step into the realm of triumphant, eternal glory—sons of God!

And may I gently remind you that anything that can be thought, can be fulfilled or brought forth? The mind cannot possibly conceive of anything that is impossible to fulfill. When the mind reaches out to fulfill the promises, all things will be accomplished and all powers be bestowed. "All things are possible to him who believes!" No one can BE and LIVE the great, almost incomprehensible promises, without fulfilling them!

Come! Travel along this glorified highway of Light into immortality, as you become love—the divine, glorified essence of all that is beautiful and lovely and desirable— members of the great Assembly of Light—even sons of God!

A MAN'S SEARCH FOR HIS SOUL

Chapter II

"And if a man should gain the whole world and lose his own soul, of what profit would it be?"

What is a man's soul? Where does it abide? How is it contacted? And above all, what is its worth if the world itself is trash in comparison?

In partial analysis it could be said that a man's soul is the realm of his own being, where the spark of God is held in an embryonic state until awakened by the conscious awareness of man. The great Creator, who is designated in scripture as our "Heavenly Father," is the Divine Sire of every earth-born child. Within each being has been implanted a spark of the Supreme Creator. God Himself placed a sacred seed of Himself in the innermost center of each man's soul. "He is in the midst of all things."

In the temples of Tibet, in the monasteries of Asia, on the high Himalayan passes, and engraved in the most sacred places of Mother India, the words stand forth in reverent declaration, "The jewel is in the lotus." And in the ancient, holy teachings the lotus is the symbol of man. The lotus seed contains the exact pattern of the matured plant in perfect embryo to the most minute detail. Each petal, each leaf, the stalk and the stem are held there in perfect design. Even the fabulous colors are contained within that seed. And so it is the soul of man embraces the perfect pattern of his own individual destiny.

This fore-ordained pattern is not a predestined arrangement for it can be altered and changed by man himself. It can be completely rejected or ignored. Or it can be enhanced and glorified according to the individual's choosing. When man permits that pattern contained within the sacred jewel of his own soul to come forth, he will be fulfilled or filled full of the glory of his own creation— "The glory which he had before the world was." It is within the lotus blossom, himself, that the perfect jewel, the divine spark of God is contained.

The soul is that knowing center within which holds all the answers to one's outside problems and inner questing. It holds the real joy that increases but never diminishes. It is the source of all inspiration and contains the power of all achievement and happiness.

The soul is the innermost being of man himself.

The soul is contacted when one learns "to be still!" When one's mind finds those sacred moments in which to withdraw from the outside activities of this crowded, hectic, outer world, he will develop the power to listen to the inner questioning that must find its answers. He will begin to get acquainted with himself during these silent periods of reverent reverie.

If one will use his power of thought to become tranquil, turning his wandering attentions inward away from life's hustle and bustle and disturbing intensity, he will begin to be instructed by God Himself.

The soul is more speedily contacted through adoring love and sincere worship as one lifts his thoughts in praise to God. True devotion discards the outer burden of earthly rituals. True devotion eliminates all restraining walls, all pretences and hypocricy. In fact, the soul is fed and nourished through the divine food of man's own tender thoughts and loving awareness. The soul matures through man's own compassionate love. The soul becomes established as one learns to focus his attention upon it. The growth of the soul and one's blending his physical body into it until they become one, contains the meaning and purpose of this life.

The voice of the soul is first heard through the voice of a man's conscience. The soul also speaks through that inner voice of praise and approval that exalts into that rapturous "good feeling." The "Still Small Voice" is never *heard*. It is *felt*. It speaks from within whenever one breaks the law of his own nature either in word or act. It speaks also whenever one performs some noble act, without expecting a reward. It is felt whenever one renders some service or sacrifices some desire that another might be benefited. It proclaims its approval whenever one triumphs over some temptation. This divine voice is the loving encouragement of the soul bearing witness, not only to the intellect but to one's entire being, that he is approved. This voice, that is *felt* instead of *heard* is called "The Still Small Voice." It is "still" because no words are uttered. Yet the lash of its rebuke can be louder than thunder, while the tenderness of its acceptance can be sweeter than a mother's lullaby. It is the "Still" voice because it makes no uttered sound. It's message is released through vibration, which is the reality back of every thought and every word. It is the true reality.

There are soulless ones who are wandering over the earth, blundering and inept, empty and alone or dangerously wicked as they live out their lives without contact with any higher help than their own mediocre, inadequate strength and understanding. These soulless ones have been deserted and left bleak and alone because of their own willingness to transgress and their own evils.

Sometimes a man sells his soul for a few bleak, empty years of worldly power or a bankfull of money, or even a few grubby coins that will be pried from his clutching fingers when his dull, physical body is finally forced to relinquish all claim to life. Those whose souls have deserted them are often found in the mental hospitals. They are also found among the deserters as they abandon the ranks of the living to become suicides, slinking away into the darkness, snatching a coward's escape.

The worth of a man's soul? One has but to contemplate the beings who have forfeited so priceless a gift to comprehend its worth. It is more precious than the diamond stardust of the Milky Way and the riches of many worlds. Within the soul is contained all the power that is, even all the dynamic powers of creation. Within the soul is contained the powers for the fulness of joy, complete happiness, eternal love and progress and achievement. Within the soul is contained the very Seed of God and within that Seed is held a man's own divinity, his power of complete fulfillment, even of godhood.

The worth of your own individual soul is beyond the worth of this entire earth and all the vast riches it contains. Your soul is of inexpressible worth. Within it is contained the jewel beyond all jewels, the treasure beyond price, "which, when a man finds he sells all that he has in order to possess it!"

Yes, "If a man gain the whole world and lose his own

soul" his hands will be empty indeed and his existence be a thing of naught or even detriment.

That jewel beyond all price contained within a man's soul is the spark or seed of God, the Almighty Father, the Divine Creator of heaven and of earth and all that in them are. It is the gift beyond all other gifts. Within it is contained the enhancing, breathtaking beauty of all crea· tion and all power. Within it is contained all perfection, all joy, all fulfilment and completion and all knowledge and good. It does not contain the power to conquer others, which is negative. It contains the positive powers of un- limited happiness and progress and everlasting joy. Within this divine gift is contained the power to bless continually, to glorify, to lift and to exalt all things and all conditions connected with one's own existence as he uses it to en- fold others in his love. As one brings forth this most priceless gem, the seed of God held within his soul, he becomes a very part of the great love of God, as it fills his being, then flowing forth from him it will help heal and bless a world.

Within the soul of man is the gift of poise, which is divine majesty. Within the soul of man is the power to rule over every condition or vicissitude. Anyone who ful- fills the law of his own being will release the full out- flowing power of God right within himself and then "all things will be subjected unto him, both in heaven and on earth; the Light and the Life; the Spirit and the Power." He will be filled with Light and comprehend all things. Such a one becomes a sacred channel through which the healing powers of God's almighty love flow out to renew in the fulness of life more abundant, joy more exquisite and knowledge more complete. Within this sacred jewel

is the power to accomplish every noble task, to fulfill every
worthy assignment and to bring forth every righteous desire. Within the soul of man is the power to KNOW and
to walk with God. Within this sacred power of the soul
is held the gift of Life Eternal, "For it is given to abide
in you the record of heaven; the Comforter, the peaceable
things of immortal glory; that which quickeneth all things,
which maketh alive all things; that which knoweth all
things and hath all power."

When man turns within and begins the quest, or the
search for his own soul, God will take care of all outside
conditions and then one will no longer need to battle and
labor for the necessities of life. "He who seeks first the
kingdom of God," or the kingdom of heaven, which is
within, "will have all things added unto him" and all
powers. He will need to take no thought about what he
will wear or what he will eat for all these things will be
provided from the great universal storehouse of living,
eternal substance. They will be formed from the "substance of things hoped for," which contains the limitless
supply of energy and atoms that fill the great immensity
of space. This divine material will be gathered into form
according to the individual's need. "And Solomon, in all
his glory, was not arrayed as one of these," for their apparel is woven of the living vibrations of everlasting light,
spun upon the loom of God.

The atoms that fill the limitless reaches of space can
and will be instantly at his command and can be gathered
into the elements and materials for his every need. His
own purified desires will form the mold or pattern into
which these precious atoms, or "substance of things hoped
for" rush together, congealing into tangible form to fulfill

his requests. This is the law of the higher kingdom, or the kingdom of heaven, which is within. These precious powers and gifts are awaiting man's acceptance of them as he grows into the glory of his waiting soul.

This embraces the realm of higher vibration which is contacted through praise and love and obedience that has become an exalted power of joy as it blends completely into the divine will of God. This obedience is not a blind, sacrificing misery. It is a glorified "willing" as it yields its essence of breathtaking, perfected love. It disperses darkness as it triumphs over all negation.

Christ gave the keys for the opening of that magic door of the soul, but none have *believed*, hence none have fulfilled the promises. None have been able to even perform the works which He did, let alone go on to the greater works. The seal on that stone door of the heart, which has caused such unyielding hardness, has remained unopened because the great Christ Light has been held entombed within each man's soul.

Christ proclaimed, "I stand at the door and knock and if any man hear my voice and open the door, behold I will come in and feast with him, and he with me." And the sacred food on which they will feast will be the very bread of life—the spiritual food in which a man will never again hunger, either physically or spiritually for all things will be added unto him.

It is the bread of life, "Which if a man eats thereof he will never die!" Which truth is verified in Christ's tender words to Martha as she grieved over the death of her brother, "Whosoever liveth and believeth in me shall never die. Believest thou this?" Then to prove His words he called Lazarus forth from the tomb.

If one professes to believe yet does not actually BE LIVE according to his professing he is a liar and a hyprocrite and all is vain. Belief is not a dead, inactive principle of mere mental or verbal confessing or professing. Belief is a way of life. It necessitates that one *BE* and *LIVE* accordingly.

Anyone who lives the teachings will have the power to fulfill them for this is the eternal, unfailing law of Jesus Christ, Son of the Living God. And "Nothing is impossible to him who believes."

When man accepts the teachings of the Savior of the world, not in a powerless affirmation of beautiful words, but by actually living the teachings he will KNOW of their truth—and "knowledge is power!" He will be able to use all the unspeakable powers contained in Christ's words of eternal, unfailing promise and so fulfill them. As those words of glory abide in the individual and are so fulfilled, that person will also become the WORD!

Or, as the writer of the Odes of Solomon testified: "Or who can rest on the most High, so that with His mouth, he may speak? Who is able to interpret the wonders of the Lord? For he who could interpret would be dissolved and would become that which is interpreted." (Lost Books of the Bible—ODES OF SOLOMON 26; 10-12).

So it is that as a man begins the greatest search of all time—the search for his own soul he will find God. "And this is life eternal, to know Thee, the only true and Living God, and Jesus Christ Whom Thou hast sent."

When one finds his own soul he will realize that the soul is developed and brought forth from its tomb through his own searching. It is not to be found through outside rituals, in great cathedrals nor in splendid synagogues, nor in churches. Neither is it found within the tenets of man's wrangling forms of worship nor learned doctrines delivered in rhetorical grandeur. The great quest for a man's soul is the quiet quest that will lead to God. It is a silent, sacred quest in which a man learns to enter the sacred closet of his own heart and there hold holy communion with the Creator of the Universe.

That divine search fulfills man's conquest of himself as he begins to live the laws, or according to the rules prescribed for his initiation into the higher world or a higher dimension. As one learns "To love God with all his heart, all his soul, all his mind and all his strength," he begins to find the joy and the meaning of existence. All fanaticism falls away as a divine, compassionate, understanding love automatically begins to fill his heart for his neighbor and for the world.

It becomes a simple thing, in fact, a necessary act for one to pray for those who have despitefully used him and for those who have considered themselves to be his enemies. As his own love increases he acknowledges no man as an enemy for his love enfolds them all. And in this love the great healing comes—first to himself—then it reaches out to those he loves, through mortal ties, and expanding on it flows out to include the whole wondrous race of man!

In this great forgiveness one's own transgressions are forgiven and though they have been as scarlet they will become white as snow.

This great perfection is not a condition into which one steps in an instant. One has to *be* it and *live* it. Then in and through him the law and the promises will be proved and fulfilled and all the holy words of God, given since

time began, will be gathered into one and be confirmed
in power and breathtaking glory. Such is the law and such
is the power thereof.

Never since time began has the challenge for man to
seek to know his own soul been so great. Never has man's
opportunities been so close at hand. Never has a time for
spiritual progress been so propitious, except at the time
of Christ's own advent on this earth.

"Ask and you shall receive! Seek and you shall find!
Knock and it shall be opened unto you! For everyone who
asks receives! And he who seeks finds! And unto him who
knocks it shall be opened!" Such is God's eternal promise
to the children of men.

Individual man has never shouldered the responsibility
of so great a work. The quest for his own soul has been
indifferently, ignorantly or fanatically placed in the hands
of some accepted leader, if undertaken at all. Man has
searched collectively and in groups in an irresponsible way.
Man has sought for his soul and for God through some
church of his choice or some religious representative. This
search is one which no man can make for another. It is a
quest which each individual must undertake for himself.
It is each individual's own responsibility. Where the scriptures enjoin man to meet together often and partake of
His holy sacrament, does not necessarily mean to gather
in meeting-houses or churches. It means that each individual is to meet together with God often—meet together
with Him in the secret closet of his own soul and there
partake of the hidden bread of Life. This is the sacred,
holy communion that will reveal the Christ. At first this
contact is only the contact with that dynamic "Christ Light
that is given to abide in every man who cometh into the

world." Then as one shuts out the world his own thoughts and mind will begin to blend with the mind and will of God. With such holy communion the individual will begin to be rewarded openly for the physical world will begin to take on the aspect of the Spiritual. This inner contact IS the "Holy Communion!" It is the partaking of the sacred bread and waters of life—even the life more abundant.

Humanity, as individuals, has relinquished its divine quest, its sacred search for the Holy Grail to its appointed religious leaders, who have themselves more often remained blind as in blindness they lead their blind followers.

Man himself is the holy chalice, the sacred grail in which the divine Eucharist is held, or from which it is bestowed. It is through and out of man's own heart that the streams of living waters must flow.

The time is at hand when each individual must meet the challenge to undertake the search for his own soul. It is the greatest quest of all time and the most rewarding. None can undertake or accomplish this search for another. It is a road of individual effort and individual desiring and individual experience. It is as individual as being born—or of dying. It pertains to the one.

He who undertakes this greatest of all quests—and continues in it, cannot possibly go unrequitted. As he becomes more and more faithful to the call of his soul and to the secret meetings within his own secret closet, as he learns to close that silent door and "be still", his own desires become purified and all promises become real and possible. As he lays hold upon them with his mind they will be fulfilled unto him. His physical being will be purified, cleansed and exalted and all outward conditions begin to serve his ennobled purposes. This is the reward that will come openly and continue to increase until every promise is fulfilled unto him. His very body will become spiritualized in time. Thus he becomes filled with light and with knowledge. He begins to comprehend all things as his vision expands and his enjoyments increase.

This quest is the most joyous search in all existence. It eliminates all darkness, all negation, all hates, all sanctimonious hyprocisy and increases the ecstatic joys until there is scarcely room enough to contain the glory singing in his soul.

As one continues in this sacred quest he will lose the grubby, little mortal "self' for his own soul, at last released, will step forth to rule and, reign in divine majesty and everlasting joy. The Light held within will be released from its tomb as the embryoed spark or seed of God develops in power to do the works which Christ proclaimed— "even the greater works."

Anyone who completes the search for his own soul will know fully, as Christ so definitely promised, that he does abide in God and that God does abide in him.

As that seed of God is developed (even as a mustard seed) one receives of its fullness. "And to know the love of Christ, which passeth knowledge, and be filled with the fulness of God!" (Eph. 3:19)

This promised "Fulness of God" is not something that is poured into a man from without. It is the divine spark that must be developed and brought forth from within until it fills the entire being of the individual who learns to *be live* in It!

"And no man receiveth a fulness unless he keepeth His commandments." These commandments are the laws of the higher kingdom. No one can abide in that kingdom unless he learns to be obedient to the laws which govern it. He must *be live* them. This obedience is not to satisfy the dictatorial demands of a domineering, temperamental God. These laws, or edicts, are for man's own progress and glory as he becomes *willing* and love filled. "He that keepeth His commandments receiveth truth and light until he is glorified in truth and knoweth all things!"

Man himself is the Holy Chalice or Grail! He is the container of the sacred sacrament. It is as he cleanses not only the outside of the cup, but the inside also that he becomes a suitable container for the fulness of the Light of Christ and the great, promised glory, even "The fulness of God!"

In this inner cleansing, one's desires automatically become purified and refined. As one follows the call of his own soul he will move towards its release and its divine maturity. His soul will be liberated as he seeks to become associated with it or makes an effort to become "one with it."

As one approaches the realm of his soul, which is perfection, his vision expands to encompass the wonders of eternity. His understanding is enlarged to comprehend all things and this "knowledge is power." As he develops into the maturity of his soul his joys increase until the earth itself cannot hold the singing vibrations of ecstatic happiness released from his own heart. To receive the fulness of God one also receives a fulness of joy and this joy can never be diminished nor withdrawn after it is once established. There is no darkness in it, no evil and no dismays. There is only the ever unfolding glory of eternal progress and increased advancement.

As one *be-lives* the higher laws of glory he leaves all bickering, bigotry and discords bèhind. All failures are

conquered. All darkness is dispelled. Joys increase in an
ever unfolding delight. As one *be-lives* the higher laws,
instead of just lending an ear to them, he sets his foot
upon the path of dynamic, unspeakable power. The Golden
Rule and the Sermon on the Mount are not impossible
teachings. Within them is contained all the love and power
that man can use as he begins to bring them forth.

SEDUCIVE SADNESS

Chapter III

The following quotation is from Hermas and was re-corded in the Lost Books of the Bible, which are no longer lost. This Hermas was the one mentioned by Paul in Romans 16:14. He was a bishop of Phillippi and a Grecian convert. Below is a portion of his conversation with the angel or shepherd instructor sent from God.

1. "Put all sadness far from thee; for it is the sister of doubting and anger. How Sir, said I (to the angel), is it the sister of these? For sadness, and anger, and doubting, seem to be very different from one another.

2. "And he answered; Art thou without intelligence that thou dost not understand? For sadness is the most mischievous of all spirits, and the worst to the servants of God; It destroys the spirits of all men, and torments the Holy Spirit . . . .

3. ". . . . . Hear, said he, and understand They who never sought out the truth, nor inquired concerning the majesty of God, but only believed (as they were told by others), are involved in the affairs of the world."

13. "But they that have the fear (awe or adoration) of the Lord, and search out the truth concerning God, having all their thoughts towards the Lord, apprehended whatsoever is said to them, and forthwith understand it, because they have the love of the Lord in them.

14. "For where the Spirit of the Lord dwells, there is also much understanding added. Wherefore join thyself to the Lord, and thou shalt understand all things.

15. "Learn now, O unwise man! How sadness troubleth the Holy Spirit. When a man that is doubtful is engaged in any affair, and does not accomplish it by reason of his doubting, this sadness enters into him, and grieves the Holy Spirit."

18. "Remove therefore sadness from thyself, and afflict not the Holy Spirit which dwelleth in thee, lest he entreat God, and depart from thee. For the Spirit of the Lord which is given to dwell in the flesh, endureth no such sadness.

19. "Wherefore clothe thyself with cheerfulness, which has always favor with the Lord, and thou shalt rejoice in it. For every cheerful man does well; and relishes those things that are good, and despises sadness.

20. "But the sad man does always wickedly. First he doeth wickedly because he grieveth the Holy Spirit, which is given to man, being of a cheerful nature. And again he doeth ill, because he prays with sadness unto the Lord, and maketh not a first thankful acknowledgement unto Him for His mercies, and obtains not of God what he asks.

21. "For the prayer of a sad man hath not the efficacy to come up to the altar of God. And I said unto him, Sir, why has not the prayer of a sad man virtue to come up to the altar of God? Because, said he, that sadness remaineth in his heart.

22. "When therefore a man's prayer shall be accompanied with sadness, it will not suffer his request to ascend pure to the altar of God. For as wine it is mingled with vinegar and has not the sweetness it had before; so sadness being

mixed with the Holy Spirit, suffers not a man's prayer to be the same as it would be otherwise.

23. "Wherefore cleanse thyself from sadness, which is evil, and thou shalt live unto God. And all others shall live unto God, as many as shall lay aside sadness and put on cheerfulness." (II Hermas 10).

The preceding quotations are definitely confirmed by Malachi in chapter two, verse thirteen of his glorious work. 'And this ye have done again, covering the altar of the Lord with tears, with weeping, and with crying out, insomuch that He regardeth not the offering any more or receiveth it with good will at your hand."

Also has God given this scriptural admonition to this world of men: "Verily, I say unto you, my friends, fear not, let your hearts be comforted; yea, rejoice evermore, and in everything give thanks!"

Or as Christ Himself admonished: "Let not your heart be troubled; neither let it be afraid."

Again, returning to the Lost Books of the Bible and to the divinely beautiful Odes of Solomon, that inspired writer has this to reveal: "Joy is of the saints! And who shall put it on, but they alone?" (Ode 23:1)

In the sixth Ode this dynamic revealer proclaimed: "As the hand moves over the harp, and the strings speak so speaks in my members the Spirit of the Lord, and I speak by His love. For it destroys what is foreign, and everything that is bitter (or sad); for thus it was from the beginning and will be to the end, that nothing (of evil vibrations) should stand up against him.

"And the Lord has multiplied the knowledge of Himself, and is zealous that these things should be known, which by His grace have been given to us. And the *Praise of His Name* He gave us; our spirits praise His Holy Spirit.

"For there went forth a stream and became a river great and broad; for it flooded and broke everything and it brought (water—even the water of life) to the Temple; and the restrainers of the children of men were not able to restrain it, nor the arts of those whose business it is to restrain waters. For it spread over the face of the whole earth and filled everything: and all the thirsty upon earth were given to drink of it; and thirst was relieved and quenched: for from the most High the draught was given.

"Blessed then are the ministers of that draught who are entrusted with that water of His: they have assuaged the dry lips, and the will that had fainted they have raised up; and souls that were near departing they have caught back from death; and limbs that had fallen they straightened and set up: They gave strength for their feebleness and light to their eyes; for everyone knew them in the Lord, and they lived by the water of life forever. Hallelujah!"

So declared one, who long ago was exalted and lifted from mortality into immortality without tasting death.

In the beginning of his fifteenth Ode the gracious revealer proclaims: "I have put on incorruption through His name; and have put off corruption by His grace. Death hath been destroyed before my face; and Sheol hath been abolished by my word; and there hath gone up deathless life in the Lord's land, and hath been made known to His faithful ones, and hath been given without stint to all those that trust in him."

And again: "I put off darkness (sadness, fear, despair and hate) and *clothed myself* with light, and my soul acquired a body free from sorrow, or affliction or pain. And increasingly helpful to me was the thought of the Lord, and His fellowship in incorruption!"

Such is God's message to man! Such has it always been! Rejoice! Praise and give thanks! Glorify God in your gladness and you will have power to rend the veil of darkness and will henceforth be clothed in Light.

Worship God! And with every singing thought of devotion praise as you watch the evils melt away and disappear. Worship and adore and let your songs of inner gratitude ascend to Him and you will soon know that you are one of the chosen ones praising at his very throne. These are the ones who have "overcome" by the glory of their love. Your song, as it wings its way forth from the fulness of your own overflowing heart, will be the "New Song." This is the song that none can learn but the righteous. It is not a song of words. It is the song of gratitude and love and praise as it ascends from the opened glory of human hearts. It is the triumphant, singing symphony of creation—the melodious harmonizing of all the glorious vibrations released from the advancing souls of men. It is the symphony of glory and gladness and love and praise and wondrous gratitude! It is the great creative, exuberant song of eternal triumph.

By learning to participate in the releasing of this unspeakable melody of unutterable glory you may take hold of the powers of creation. And by so doing you need never again know want or despair nor pain and distress for all these things will be done away in you. "For all things will be subject unto you, both the Light and the Life; the Spirit and the Power, sent forth by the will of the Father, through Jesus Christ, His Son!"

Joy, which is the opposite of sadness, is a very spiritual

condition. "A fulness of joy" which is promised in the scriptures, is a fulness of life. It is life expressed in its fullest extent. It is the "life more abundant, even Life Eternal.

"Fulness of joy" is also used synonomously with the promise of "Fulness of God!" Which is the ultimate completion of all that is glorious and perfect and sublime and powerful.

Singing gratitude and praise brings forth this great gift of joy more speedily and more completely than any other attitude or method possible to apply. Praise and give thanks and rejoice and sorrow will flee from you. It will be dissolved along with the veil of darkness as you step forth into the singing wonder of His divine, holy Light.

Remember always, in the moment of Christ's greatest suffering He was offered the "bitterness and gall." He rejected it. He could have given way to His human heritage and wallowed in the bitterness and the gall of injustice and sobbed in his self-pity. So can you. Or you, like Christ, can reach beyond mortality into the God-given powers of your own soul and reject the low, mortal thoughts of bitterness and gall as you rise triumphant forever over every disastrous calamity or misfortune.

LIFE MORE ABUNDANT!

Chapter IV

"That you might have life, and have it more abundantly—even the gift of Life Eternal!"

Life itself is a sparkling fountain of abundant, joyous, intelligent vitality. It is an everlasting power of beauty and renewal when comprehended. Life is a very sacred gift and was not intended to be neglected nor squandered. Neither was it meant to be dissipated nor destroyed. Life was never intended to be taken for granted or resented, as I once resented it. Life itself contains all that is whole and beautiful and complete and glorious when one becomes aware of its eternal vibrancy, its exulting, exuberating, triumphant song of BE-ING.

Vibrant, interesting, attractive people are those who are literally vibrating with aliveness. Vibrant means to vibrate with life. Vibrant people are those who are tingling with the vital forces of divine life surging within themselves in an aware alertness of activity. This is not the out-side, running to and fro activity but the dynamic, powerful activity of intelligence and purpose as one "STANDS FORTH" to fulfill the highest good within himself.

Those who are dull, uninteresting, boring and completely unanimated or in a state of half-dead zombieism are the ones who are, or have, permitted the life force to be crowded out of their bodies by negligence, ignorance, accepted nurtured sorrows, or indifference. These are the ones who have never understood nor valued the singing power of abundant life nor reached for that promised "Life Eternal." They have never thrilled with the glory of breathing, the dynamic power of thinking, the sublime wonder of actually *being* alive! They have never dreamed that they were intended to become the masters of that vibrant life-force surging within themselves. They may have even resented, at times, a gift so priceless and hence they have not appreciated it. They have never been really aware of the full purpose and power of that dynamic force of life right within themselves and hence have failed to make full use of its immeasurable powers. Within this precious gift of life is the power of complete mastery over one's self.

Those who have failed to bring forth the full power of life, have failed to realize that it all lies in their power of choice as they select or fail to make a selection of their own thoughts. The very power to select one's thoughts is the heritage of gods.

When one begins to comprehend the power of the great life-force within and begins to make a selection of the thoughts that are permitted to abide within his mind, then all evil, desolating, negative thoughts can be rejected. Darkness can be banished forever. Vibrant, glorious life is then released within one's own being with its full, flowing power of exultation. One can then direct the flow of life within and thereby increase its everlasting powers of triumphant exuberance.

The divine privilege of the gift of Life is the very power of existence! It is the joy of *being!* It is a privilege so sacred and so breathtaking it is almost beyond thought. And certainly it is beyond the power of words to reveal. Life

itself holds within it the power of continual renewing, if
one but permits it to come forth. Each moment holds a
new beginning. Each day nurtures a promised marvel of
singing fulfilment. Each breath contains within it the
promise of new hope and greater accomplishments in the
unspeakable magnitude of eternal, ever increasing triumphs.

Life is the dynamic, sublime gift of BEING. Within it
is held all the unspeakable powers of existence. It is a
privilege and also a responsibility. Just as wealth and high
positions carry with them greater obligations and responsibilities so does the precious gift of life carry with it certain duties and obligations. Few have ever understood or
accepted the divine responsibilities entrusted to them along
with that precious heritage of life—hence many tread the
earth with death cavorting triumphantly at their heels in
mocking derision even as it rides in-waiting upon the unholy man's coat-tails.

There is a deep obligation that goes with the sacred gift
of life. Every human being who comes into this world was
intended to help make it a better place to live in because
he was permitted to live here. Each is expected to live according to the very highest impulses of his own divine nature. None are exempted from this requirement—and every
living soul will be held accountable. And sometimes the
greatest wickedness of all is the bitter intolerance that has
been prepetuated under the guise of "righteousness," or
some man-interpreted form of religion. The service one is
required to render to this world is in helping to make it a
better place in which to live, not just for a few, but for all.

Occasionally those who have been restored to life, or
had their lives spared by a seeming miracle, appreciate the
gift, at least for awhile. But even they often forget the

wondrous marvel and blessing in being permitted to retain this one reality with which they have been so generously endowed.

No life came into being through accident. Every individual was a son or daughter of God before he was ever entrusted into the care of his mortal parents. Every individual's life was bequeathed to him in the beginning as a priceless, irreplaceable gift. However, many lives have become quite worthless, either to themselves, or to the world or to God through their own actions or because of their negative re-actions and hence the divine heritage so generously given has slipped from their grasp as they are left bleak and desolate and naked.

There is another truth that must be mentioned here: the more worthless a life has become, through transgression, selfishness and lustful evils and vicious crimes, the harder will the individual fight to maintain his hold upon it. Why? Simply because within him is the instinctive knowledge that if he loses his life, through failure, he will lose all. So it is a coward will permit an innocent man to die in his place, or let another receive the punishment for his crimes as he clutches the ragged shreds of that which he has already so ignominiously forfeited.

Yet it is true that, "as long as there is life there is hope." This is more true than anyone realizes. As long as there is the breath of life within one there is the opportunity to use that breath aright—and within that breath is held the power of new beginnings.

Life is a gift that increases its glowing, unfolding, innumerable blessings and powers by awareness and appreciation of its unutterable, glorious majesty.

Thrill with the gift of Life and let its tingling, reverberating power surge through your being with awakening vitality. Let your own awareness of its invigorating forces increase continually.

"He who loves his life shall lose it and he who hates his life shall find it," does not mean the great God principle of existence but the mediocre mortal existence one casually accepts with all its physical entrappings. This scripture is not referring to the great, vibrant Spirit of exquisite, dynamic power held within the confines of a man's soul. This Life principle is of God and is enhanced by love and appreciation and praise.

The more aware one is to the vibrating gift of life the more powerful will become his thoughts, the more dynamic his nature and his actions and the more beautiful will be his life. As one's appreciation for the gift of life increases, the powers of God will be released more fully and with greater abundance into his physical being.

No individual can possibly be dull, uninteresting or a failure who appreciates the sacred gift of life and then lives worthy of so holy a bequest.

"The life more abundant—yes—even Life Eternal" is only the consciousness or awareness of the value of so precious a legacy. With comprehension one can develop his life into an ever increasing rhythm of singing, triumphant splendor.

Life becomes a living fountain of increasing joy that multiplies into delights in a wondrous unfolding of everlasting radiance by simply being grateful for it. Joy itself is LIFE! And life is love and harmony and beauty immeasurable. Beauty is life's glorious expression. Youth is its reality. Joy is its language. And singing gratitude and praise hold the keys of its eternal release.

As the gift of inner life is taken hold of and reveled in the body begins to take on the effulgence of everlasting, deathless beauty and vitality.

The body grows old through negative thinking. Thought by thought the body assumes the vibrational reactions of every discord, every fear, every dismal, hateful, jealous, sorrowful, self-pitying idea harbored in the mind of man. Thoughts reveal their secrets on the open surface of the face and skin. From thoughts and emotions come the etchings of time as each line is engraved by the mis-use of the powers of one's own thoughts. Wrinkles with all their ugly tracings write their own story upon the human countenance and form. Evil thoughts are the saboteurs of youth and beauty, and of life itself.

There is no room for the ugliness of age, the negation of disease or the decay of death to take hold as long as one revels in the gift and blessing of life. And for such a one life becomes ever more abundant. As one rejoices and gives thanks for the divine, wondrous gift of life, his life forces will be increased instead of being diminished within him.

"Life more abundant" belongs to all who will only accept, with appreciation, the divine heritage bequeathed to them by God. Such will begin to participate in the infinite powers of that divine life.

Mortal man has fully accepted the human side of his nature in a fullness of acquiescence. And in so doing he has ignored the spiritual side of his nature almost entirely. He has walked the path of earth harboring the negative, grubby thoughts of the flesh—the thoughts of fear, dislikes, hates and morbid-mindedness—the thoughts that lead to death. Occasionally he may attend some Sunday service to glimpse for a brief moment a higher way. But always he returns again, though mayhap with an inward sigh of regret, to the habitual road of trudging mortals. Yet in that moment of Sabatical delight some noble thought, lingering, may help sustain him in unknown ways for hours or even days to come.

Old age is no longer to be a thing of days or years. Age is a condition registered by thought and mortal concepts. Old age is the backward look as it squanders the present. Old age is the backward look that gathers into its fold all the mortal fears and failures and follies and discords of the past. Old age holds to the ancient discordant hates and resentments, to the marred moments of anguish, the pains and sufferings and sorrows, keeping them forever alive, as they become permanently engraved into the perfect smoothness of the skin. Age is but the etching on the face of memory's anguished, hateful thoughts. Age is that backward look that clings to the mistakes and the sorrows and the griefs that were meant to pass away after their lesson was learned.

Old age is an ugly thing. It is a false condition. Fortunes have been and are being spent to erase its ugly script from the faces of women. They may have their faces "lifted" by painful, intricate, expensive operations that leave a greater weakness for those muscles to sag into the rhythm of their established thinking patterns.

The only permanent "lifting", which is not contrary to natural laws, is the uplifting of one's own thoughts. As one learns to think only the most beautiful things possible, holding himself in the joyous vibrating existence of that ever-present, glorious NOW, the realm of the soul, his face will be lifted to correspond with his thoughts.

The ancient engraving may not be changed in a day. It took years to establish that distorted pattern known as "AGE". But it can be changed thought by thought as all negation is overcome through exalted thinking habits. Wrinkles are but the dried excrements of the mind. And as the wonderful revealer of the Odes of Solomon wrote in his thirteenth Ode: "Tell forth praise to His Spirit: and *wipe off the filth from your face*: and love his holiness, and clothe yourself therewith."

As one lets only love and kindness pour forth from his heart and his mind he learns to hold himself in the great stream of God's concentrated love and will receive the life more abundant and will be restored to beauty, both of form and feature.

None have ever *believed* His teachings, hence none have ever received the "Life more abundant." The very principle of life diminishes as an individual permits the great life force, so sacredly entrusted to him, to be slowly extracted by contrary thinking and feeling habits.

"EXISTENCE" is from the latin words meaning literally to "STAND FORTH!" This is the life more abundant! It is the dynamic, living, pulsating force of life in constant and continual action as its powers and energies are renewed, regenerated and released from within. It is the love of God that is shed forth through the hearts of the children of men. And one can literally bathe himself in this divine love of God whenever he so desires. More will be given upon this matter later.

Love is life! One can become that love as he permits it to flow out through his being to enfold the world and every living thing upon it. In this outpouring love one's own soul is the first to receive of its healing, maturing, glorifying powers of renewal and quickening. Next the physical body will be enchanced as one is rewarded openly for his own inner communion. Then it is that this love, in expanding and increasing grandeur and power, will flow out through his heart to help heal and bless a world.

This love of God holds within its potential powers the power to "lift" and exalt not only one's face but every condition. This love is brought forth through man's own thinking and "feeling" vibrations and activities. As one's thinking is exalted the face will be lifted to assume the loveliness and beauty of his thoughts. His body will also be enhanced as his entire being casts aside the secret shadows his mind has embedded into it through his mortal mis-thinking.

Haggard, aged countenances are caused by negative, discordant thoughts, not by time, though it does take time to engrave such dismal lines into the living tissues of man's flesh.

As one steps into the "Life More Abundant," by his exalted vision, the lower laws of mortal, negative thinking will be replaced by the love and power of divine thinking. The body will become the holy instrument through which the soul operates as the love of God is released in ever increasing beauty to fill the entire being of man. Then the whole body becomes enhanced, beautified, invigorated, renewed and glorified. The physical part of man, the mortal flesh, assumes the powers of the Spirit as he becomes alive to "STAND FORTH" in the power of God—to be fulfilled! This is man's destiny and his true heritage. From the most humble mortal to the highest monarch it is the same. The law is eternal and the way of Life is established.

Rejoice in every noble aspect or glimpse that opens to

your mental view. Make an effort to fight the lethargy
that would lull you back into stupid existence, ruled by
your old thought patterns and habits, if you do not make
a stand. Many of the old, accepted thoughts were established
generations ago and man is still accepting them. Man must
lift himself to behold the things of the Spirit.

As the spiritual side of one's nature is accepted and
developed, through appreciation and belief, man is automatically lifted into a higher vibrational existence. And
within the Spirit is the gift of life. This life becomes more
abundant, more vibrant and powerful with one's increasing awareness of it.

Within man himself lies the choice of selection as he
travels the road toward his own goals.

> "There is a way—and ways—and THE WAY!
> And the high man travels the high way,
> And the low man travels the low—
> While in between, on the misty flats, the rest
>   drift to and fro.
> But for every man that goeth,
> There's a high way and a low—
> And every man decideth the way his soul
>   shall go!"

There is the road of life and there is the road of old age
and death. And in between there are "illions" of inviting,
subtle, deceptive little by-roads, all eventually emerging
into the great beaten path that leads to that ugly back door
of death.

The road of life is ignored because it is not wide nor
broad. And at first it appears to be too difficult and steep.
It takes vision and determination to travel it, though it is

narrow and it is straight—for always the goal is right ahead. It is difficult at first because one has to climb up and out of the ruts dug deep by preceding generations with their conformed thinking habits. One must first believe there is a higher way of life than mere mediocre, mortal living. Then he must *believe* or BE and LIVE accordingly.

This journey into the higher realm is a far greater journey than Columbus took in order to span the oceans and reveal new lands of promise. It is a greater journey by far than that undertaken by our pioneer ancestors as they settled the far flung expanses of the west.

In crossing the ocean there was a boat with a tangible deck beneath their feet. There was the wide reality of the endless waters surrounding them. They were enfolded in the tangible reality of material substance. It was only in the heart of one man that a vision beckoned, clear and more real than the substantial surrounding of earthly reality. To Columbus the vision was more genuine than the ship or the ocean or the clouds. To Columbus that vision was the one great, inspiring reality.

The western pioneers also followed their dreams. They too had their tangible surroundings, their wagons, though in some instances only makeshift, unwieldly handcarts. But with all, their hands gripped hard materials and their feet trod firmly upon the solid earth.

Those who travel this greater way must do so at first through *belief*. Of them it is required to struggle not against expanses and time and hardships and privations but against the unseen forces of human habits and beliefs. The struggle is against the inherent lethargy and the mental fears and doubts that have been implanted within themselves, perhaps for centuries. Their struggle is not against great monsters waiting at the "outer edge", nor against savage Indians, nor against raging torrents nor high mountains. No. They have no such tangible difficulties to combat and overcome. Their struggles are against the darkness of unbelief, against their own morbid memories, against discords and lusts and dismays and against the corroding, lingering dislikes of years as well as against the orthodoxed walls that man has constructed around himself since time itself began. Each individual must prod himself into mental alertness.

Yet this higher road is as literal and as real as any highway on the earth. It is more so to those who have traveled it. It is a road that at first must be desired and so one needs to call on faith to verify its veiled reality. Faith is the very ingredient which lifts a man out of the doubting, worm consciousness of earthly, mortal thinking. Faith gives the mind power to soar above the dust of the beaten, earthbound track. Faith is the very power that opens one's mind to BE LIEVE as it prepares one's mental eyes to see that which is not visible to the common group.

Faith may be but the desire to rise above the sorrows, the vicissitudes and the evils of this lonely, dreary world of fears and failures and heartrending sorrows. Faith may be but an upward glance of the soul as the mind opens to question the *why* that lies behind an existence that is so drab and ugly. Faith is a hope that may burn for but a moment before being extinguished by the smothering density of mortal thinking. Yet every lifted thought, every shimmering hope, every questioning idea is the food on which faith grows and becomes established. Faith is the power that opens the mind and the heart to the great wonders of eternity. Faith is the very essence of the soul and prepares one for that secret, inner directing which comes only from God. This loving, unspeakable, inner directing is every man's right as he opens his soul to accept. And as one thus opens his soul and heart he will be individually taught of God. Such a one will need none to teach him as he learns to walk in majesty, radiating Light.

As one travels this road, that is above all others, he learns the wonder of *living* the laws Christ gave. They are no longer impossible words given to mock man. They become shining way-marks along a trail of utter glory rising in singing triumph to the highest stars.

As one accepts the higher laws and begins to apply them in his life he enters the life more abundant. In fact he takes hold of the very essence of life itself. The higher road is as much a road of letting go of old thinking habits as it is one of acquiring new information in every increasing vision of unutterable glory. The greater vision is no longer an unattainable hope. It becomes the one great, glorious reality.

As one travels this higher road of light he will soon realize that he is traveling in the Spirit. He has left the heavy task-master behind, mammon. The very earth has lost all hold upon him. He is free! Forever and forever abundantly, beautifully free! It is then one realizes that never again can he relapse or return to the caverned, dismal darkness of mortal thinking and existing. He has learned to think only the most beautiful things possible and has thereby entered a realm of sheer, exquisite beauty, of joy and gladness and everlasting, increasing power. He is abiding in the life more abundant, vibrant, exotic, eternal! He has overcome the weaknesses of the flesh. And he learns that they were all contained in his own habits of thought.

They were as deeply grooved into his mind, those strange patterns of thinking, as were the pioneer trails of long ago—and they were as solid and concrete as the great freeways of today. In overcoming the old habitual thoughts of darkness and decay and death, one steps forth into a more abundant life than he ever before dreamed possible.

In this estate, death has no claim. The body, instead of growing old and dying, is renewed and charged with the glowing, powerful, vibrating ecstasy of Life Eternal.

THE SOUL'S COMMAND

Chapter V

If one catches a glimpse of the higher way of life, the way that by-passes death and all its sordid negation, then he must open his heart and mind to new and vibrant truths.

If one can accept the truth that old age, ugliness and even death itself are but the results of man's own negative, erroneous thinking then he must begin to contemplate the reality of thoughts and begin to choose the kind he is willing to harbor. Every thought becomes more powerful when given an abode in a man's mind as it is fed and nourished upon the very essence of his own being.

As one begins to select the caliber of the thoughts he will harbor and entertain, then it is that he places his feet upon the path of higher attainment. He, in that moment, becomes a disciple for he willingly places himself under discipline.

To make the road more clear it will be necessary to reveal the way to select thoughts for often they come unbidden to find a roosting place in the rafters of one's brain. Any thought that is unworthy must be replaced instantly by a more worthy one. The mind cannot become a void. If kind, gracious, beautiful thoughts fill the mind there will be no room for morbid, disagreeable, sorrowful, lustful or evil ones. The two types cannot possibly abide together.

And man, at the end of his life, is but the sum total of

all the thoughts he has harbored and held to or sheltered in the hidden recesses of his mind. He is a great man, a mediocre man or an evil, wicked man according to his established thinking habits. Oh yes, a man's way of thinking becomes an habitual thing. And often it is more difficult to break the pattern of one's thought habits than one's personal, everyday, established physical habits.

The mind can be a wishy-washy, cluttered roosting place for every type of drifting thought that happens to drop in. This is "idle thinking" and every individual will be judged by his "idle thoughts" or those worthless thoughts his mind harbors.

Selected thoughts are never idle. And as one undertakes to select his thoughts he advances from a mediocre individual into a thinker. Few people really think. To think one has to select the type of thoughts he entertains.

The brain is a physical organ, an instrument in which the mystic entities of thoughts are harbored and nourished and kept alive.

But the mind is quite different from the brain. The brain is the organ or instrument through which the mind operates. The brain is the housing or casing for the mind just as the body is the abode or dwelling place of the spirit.

The mind is fluid. There are no realms it cannot explore. Time and space are banished by its touch. The mind is spiritual. The mind is a living thing confined neither by time nor space. The mind is a sacred, super-sensitive, almost unanalyzable apparatus of unmeasured quality and infinite power when commanded and put to correct use.

Knowledge is stored in the brain. Facts are gathered and filed away in its niches like papers are filed in the pigeon-holes of a cabinet. But the mind is not a static organ. The mind is a living essence of unlimited power. Its functioning is arbitrary for it can be mis-used as easily as it can be used correctly.

And though both the brain and the mind can be grossly and tragically misused there is within man the ability to command the hidden powers of his mind and be obeyed. Man has within himself the power to command his mind to harbor only thoughts of the highest quality. There is no limit to which man can use the power of his mind. He can use such powers to perfect his holy, divine gift of love as he develops his mind to fulfill its most excellent, positive degree of functioning as he trains it to "Love God" with all its intensity and its power. Then expanding that love he can truly love his neighbor as himself. He can eliminate every dismay, every fear-filled, antagonistic, hateful thought as joyous thoughts rush in to fill his entire being.

What power is there within man that can thus stand guardian over his mind and command it to obey? What power is there that can demand thoughts be selected—or rejected? If the mind can be used for evil as readily and as easily as it can be used for good, then what hidden force is there within man that can demand obedience from the mind and command it to obey? What hidden intelligence stands over the mind that can demand its powers be used for righteousness?

What could there possibly be higher than the mind but the soul? So it is that one must demand his soul to stand forth and take command. This is his heritage. It is the soul that has the power to command the mind and then the divine ability to see that it obeys. The spirit within man must be developed through man's acceptance and awareness of it. As it is placed on the throne of man's being, in complete command, "He whose right it is to rule"—the orders and dis-orders of the flesh are canceled and eliminated.

It is the soul that must stand forth and give the all-powerful command of creation: "LET THERE BE!" "Let there be peace! Let there be understanding! Let there be love! "Let there be Light" on any subject on which one is seeking information. Or, "Let only beautiful thoughts be permitted to enter the sacred precincts of my mind! Let all evil, negative, discordant thoughts be forever banished!" Then it is up to the individual to keep watch to see that the command is obeyed. This is the process of bringing forth—the law of creation.

The physical dominion of earth has held captive, both the minds and souls of men. "Man is born in sin" just as a fish is born in water. He is born into it and is completely surrounded by sin and negation from infancy.

Childhood and youth are spent in developing the physical body while the spiritual nature of man is almost completely ignored. Placing religious seals upon a child's mind, as he is orthodoxed and cramped into narrowed conformity by some creed or applied rituals, is not necessarily a training that develops spiritual growth. And more often than not such rigid training brings a retardment to the spontaneous development of the soul rather than assistance.

The telling of stories in some Sunday school class, stories of the exploits of the great ones of the past, is not sufficient to develop the soul of a child, nor of a man. One can only develop spiritually as his own soul is instructed and assisted in its own growth. Man must be taught how to step forth to fulfill the great works of the past—and exceed them in "The greater works!" This is man's right.

Children must be instructed how to contact and use the unspeakable powers contained right within themselves.

It is a tragic thing, yet true, that if any one stepped forth to attempt the greater works he would be crucified by the ridicule and derisive persecution of his fellow Christians.

Such magnificent thoughts as one's daring to believe in the possibility of fulfilling Christs' great and unspeakable promises in this present day and age have never been allowed to enter the minds of the children of men. So how can any one grow up with the vision and the ability to instruct the little ones in some Sunday school class as to how to go about fulfilling such irrevocable, dynamic, eternal promises? Such promises have been looked upon only through the blind, mortal eyes of the masses and the deeply veiled vision of their leaders.

Those who look only into the past to behold the miracles and the works of God and who have never lifted their eyes to behold His glory or His power in the present, have remained unenlightened and impotent and have failed Christ utterly.

No wonder "The learning of the world is foolishness to God!" The learning of the world is composed entirely of the tangible, orthodoxed works brought forth by the physical side of man's nature. Churches point into the past for their foundations and their structures. Their authority and their power is the *past* instead of the Living God. They exist in the shadows of "What has been."

The earth is flooded with books that deal in crime and sex. Paintings are actually defiling the earth in their ugly, morbid-minded distortions of the Divine Creator's handiwork. His sublime creations are smeared in ugliness as they are lauded as modern art. Entertainment has become a perverted, shocking revelation of man's lowest impulses. Nations are stacking up their desecrating instruments of war and destruction. Industries are burdened with mechanical gadgets and almost incomprehensible, cumbersome machines while man himself is more dwarfed and afraid and lost and bewildered than ever before.

It is only because of the bleak, skimped, fearful little thoughts of the physical minds of men that Christ's teachings and His dynamic promises have remained unfulfilled. The very lack of power stands as a mockery to His Holy Name. Why have not professing Christian leaders fulfilled His words proving their belief in Him? Why have these, who so loudly proclaim their belief in wordy sermons, remained so empty of power? Why do they not heal the sick, the lame, the halt and the blind and cast out devils, or the unclean spirits and thoughts harbored in the minds of the mental cases, which are increasing in such alarming numbers upon the earth? Why do they not bless the meager supply into an over-abundance?

Why? Simply because it is the over-ruling, mortal, physical side of man's nature, that does not have the ability to apply His powerful teachings of eternal, living power, that is functioning. New churches are being constructed to extort funds from the already over-burdened inhabitants of the earth as they glorify their empty altars while pointing their spired steeples upward like fingers, shaming the sky. And these same churches become only the musty, archived receptacles of past traditions instead of endowing their living members with the knowledge of how to fulfill His promises and so bring forth their own powers to stupendous accomplishment. Christian philosophy has become a rattling skeleton which is violently shaken on Sabbath days by the shouted phrases of the preachers. Yet their words are without power as they direct the minds of men back across the ages to the great *"once-was."* The powerful present, the eternal NOW is never permitted to express in the lives of the living. Man is held in profound ignorance as his attention is directed backward and veiled mystery shrouds God in an unapproachable realm of dead, by-gone power. God has been held in a realm of impotency because man has lost the power to believe in His promises and the way of their fulfilling. He has lost the contact with his own soul and hence the contact with God.

As the soul is commanded to STAND FORTH the mind is subjected to obey. As the mind is refined and trained to obey one learns to think with purpose and power. The black, hideous, nightmare thoughts, the weak, impotent thoughts as well as the greedy, jealous, or revengeful thoughts of hate and fear are conquered and eliminated. These sordid, mortal thoughts are then replaced by thoughts of singing, triumphant beauty as one's eyes become single to the dynamic, breathtaking glory of God. With the joyous vision of that perfection established in singing praise and gratitude one becomes glorious.

Oh man of a million mystic, unfathomed, subtle and unused powers, which have lain dormant within, leave your mortal thinking habits and negatious restrictions behind and step forth into the full measure of your creation.

"To be carnally minded is death, but to be spiritually minded is life and peace." It is also power. (Rom. 8:6).

The Light of Christ is the Spirit of Truth and the powers of creation are contained within. "As also the Light of

Christ is in the sun and the light of the sun and the power thereof by which it was made.

"As also he is in the moon, and is the light of the moon, and the power thereof by which it was made;

"As also the light of the stars, and the power thereof by which they were made;

"And the earth also, and the power thereof, even the earth upon which you stand.

"And the light which shineth, which giveth you light, is through him who enlighteneth your eyes, which is the same light that quickeneth your understandings;

"*Which light procedeth forth from the presence of God to fill the immensity of space—*

"The Light which is in all things, *which giveth life to all things,* which is the law by which all things are governed, even the power of God, who sitteth upon his throne, who is in the bosom of eternity. *Who is in the midst of all things.*"

When one brings forth that "Light of Christ which is given to abide in the very center or *'midst'* or middle of a man's own being," he will be in contact with truth. "He will know the Truth and will be henceforth free!"

Within that light, held unfulfilled within man's own inner being, is engraved the record of heaven. Also within that dynamic light, held entombed within his own being, is the pattern and the power of each individual's own fulfilment and the truth and the power of every promise ever given by God to man.

When that Christ Light is brought forth and developed from within It will have the ability and the power to contact that same Light that fills the great immensity of space and one will be able "to comprehend all things!" He will also be able to contact that same light in the heart of another and help to awaken it and bring it forth.

As that divine Christ Light is brought forth, through one's mind reaching out to accept and comprehend it, a man becomes one with the very fulness of that light. So it is that as an individual becomes one with that light he also becomes equal with it.

As the spirit is commanded to step forth and the mind is brought to obey, man places at the controls or helm of his own being the power of divinity and he passes from mortality into immortality.

As one learns to consult his soul in whatsoever he does instead of blundering through his dealings and his life with only his mortal, physical qualities functioning, he is lifted above the vicissitudes, temptations, afflictions and forces of this "lone and dreary world."

THE MASTER

Chapter VI

As the soul is taken into partnership the ills and evils of life are left behind. This is the "overcoming" spoken of in the seven verses of flame scattered about in the first few chapters of Revelations. This is the point where the request held forth in the Lord's Prayer; "deliver us from evil" is fulfilled. This is the point where one becomes the master of his own being instead of the weak, miserable, driven slave. This is when one begins to live according to the divine, true pattern of himself and henceforth he walks with God.

Command your soul to "STAND FORTH" in the full measure of its EXISTENCE to rule and be obeyed. You will then have the mastery over your actions and your re-actions. You will "speak no word except God commands it" or speaks through you. You will do no work without His sustaining, revealing power to ensure its success. Your words will be powerful and your actions will be majestic and un-wasted and uninjurious either to yourself or to others.

In this divine condition even the mistakes and messes of the past will be righted and eliminated. Then it is that the perfection of the present is fully established.

The whole horrifying condition of this earth, "its wars and rumors of wars," its famines and pestilences and diseases and its staggering number of ever increasing mental cases and all its uncontrolled, rampant evils are but the results of man's own selfish, lustful greeds and hates which have expressed in completion the physical, mortal side of his nature.

But man is also a spiritual being. And within the soul of every man the seed of God is held embryoed, waiting to come forth that man might be divine.

Cherubim was placed at the gate of Paradise with a flaming sword to guard the way to the Tree of Life, lest man put forth his hand and partake of the fruit of that precious tree and live forever in his sins, or live without overcoming them.

That flaming sword that flashes every-which-way is but the uncontrolled, disquieted thoughts of man as they swing out hither and yon to hold one's mind so occupied with mortal problems and conditions there is no time nor power to attend to the spiritual longings buried in the soul. And all powerful thoughts release more powerful vibrations that flash forth like two-edged swords to rend and cut down.

How can man possibly return to Paradise as long as his thoughts are uncontrolled and his vibrations are permitted to swing out in such detrimental release to block his own way back into the realm of his own perfection?

"To him who overcometh I will cause to eat of the fruit of the tree of life which is in the midst of the Paradise of God." (Rev. 2:7). And may I repeat: "The kingdom of heaven is within you."

Let the soul "STAND FORTH" in full command and all things will become subjected unto you, "The life and the light, the spirit and the power, sent forth by the will of the Father, through Jesus Christ, His Son."

As the mind is brought to obey, the body will be lifted into the light and one again has access into the Paradise of God, to take up his progressive journey to the stars.

With the selection and control of thoughts comes the control of vibrations. And vibrations are the expression of existence. Spirit is the pulsating, vibrating life force that fills the immensity of space. Light is released in its glorious vibrations of everlasting life to reveal itself to the eyes and understandings of man.

He who learns to control his thoughts through a gracious, noble mastery, as his soul STANDS guard, becomes also master of the vibrations that enter his being from the outside. He can hold the guard of love and light so firmly around himself that no destructive, harmful vibrations can possibly enter the citadel of himself from without. No other's hates can upset or disturb him. Nor can another's actions effect him in any way. With this calm self-mastery one will also have the power to protect his loved ones. By this method of love he can begin to reach out to enfold his neighbors, his associates and the world.

Such a one will have the power to control every vibration released within himself so that no angry, impatient, disturbed, evil vibrations can go forth from him to wreak their destructiveness upon the world, thus adding to the accumulated darkness already enfolding the earth.

With his thoughts thus held in control one can so enfold himself, his loved ones, if they will but permit, and the world, in the essence of his living, healing love.

Such a one can build an armor of light so powerful around himself that no evil or destroying force in existence can possibly disturb him.

In this way one gains control of the vibrations of existence and they become subjected unto him, "even the life and the light and the spirit and the power." These almost unimaginable promises, given by God to His children, hold the very forces of life within them. These are the dynamic works which Christ did—and the promises he left for us to fulfill also.

These are the works which man must begin to do that His words may not return unto Him void. Man must do all the works which Christ did and then go on to the greater works. Blasphemy you say? Not so. They are the eternal, living promises of God our Almighty Father of Love expressed through the glory and the words of His Beloved Son. They are the promises given unto us.

All commands and all promises are yours to fulfill. "And God gives no command save he opens the way for its fulfilment." And no promise was ever given that did not contain the seed of its own completion.

As a man becomes the master of his thoughts, through his soul taking command, he reaches the point where power is established. Then it is that he can step forth into his own divinity.

The promises Christ gave have remained unfulfilled because man has been satisfied to live in the darkness of his own disbeliefs or his own orthodoxed way of thinking. The promises are irrevocably established. Even God Himself cannot revoke them else He would cease to be God. And He has given His holy word, proclaiming, "When ye do as I say, then am I bound!" Could anything be more powerfully stated? God has pledged Himself to the fulfilling of His promises and they cannot fail. Neither can His word return unto Him void.

"Be ye doers of the word, and not hearers only, deceiving your own selves." (James 1:22)

Man has truly deceived himself, failed himself and most

assuredly failed his Creator. He is near to destroying the world and all that it contains by his own blind deception. He has nurtured his unbelief, his hates, his sorrows and his lusts. He has increased his greeds and his jealousies and his fears as he has kept them alive on the very substance of his own being for they have been fed and feasted on the fibres of his own mind as well as the very life essence of his soul. And man has then released these vile, over-indulged, repulsive, monstrous vibrations of darkness upon the world in the turbulent dis-quietude of his own seething resentments and unholy actions.

A man can be an animal of the flesh—or even less. Or he can be a man. But it is also possible that he can become divine according to the thoughts he harbors as he be-lives and so fulfills his beliefs.

Man is a Creator! And all that the Father has is his—to use for glory or for destruction—the sorrowful destruction of himself as he betrays his own soul, rejecting the divine, eternal gift of life and light God so graciously gave to every man who ever came into the world.

As long as a man remains subjected to the flesh and to the random or evil thoughts of his lowest, animal nature he is a slave. Only as he stands forth in the superb command of his soul does he become the master. Then he has the power to step forth into the presence of God, his divine Sire, a son of light.

The great ignorance that has held man enslaved in darkness, not daring to lift his head above the dull, mortal heritage of grubby, earthly thinking must now end. From henceforth the time is established when all men will be left without excuse.

The great New Age of Light is yours to advance into

and become one with, dynamic, glorified and in full mastery of your every faculty and power.

Come, beloved! Come into the realm where the most noble aspirations of your own soul become the reality and are fulfilled beyond your present power to even imagine.

Come! The way is yours! It is the sacred Way of Truth, the inner way of Light! This is the Straight and Narrow Way Christ IS!

"ALL THINGS WORK TOGETHER FOR GOOD
TO THEM THAT LOVE GOD"

Chapter VII

It is most assuredly true that "All things work together for Good to them that love God." (Rom. 8:28).

To fulfill this scripture and prove one's love, is quite different from quoting it in words, then denying its truth by brooding over all the evils and misfortunes you have been subjected to. Neither can it be fulfilled by those who weep in self-pity, nor whimper in dismay, over every trivial discomfort.

This scripture can be proved and fulfilled when it is put to the full test. It has to reach beyond words and superficial, sanctimonious self-righteousness. It has to reach beyond the services that one renders in the lime-light of the temple pinnacle to be seen of men.

This love for God that is required, is not something that can be proved in declarations nor even in spell-binding sermons uttered from the "housetops." Love is a power that must go out from the heart. It must be felt and comprehended as it is released in vibrations of glorious, singing aliveness.

To prove this scripture it is necessary to love God with a devotion that exceeds the little, mortal self. This love requires that one trust God implicitly. This deep, wondrous, living love provides one with the willingness to go through any testing, any vicissitude, any difficulty, no matter how seemingly impossible, with an inner song of love and praise— and gratitude.

Impossible?

Not at all.

If you really do love God, then it is quite easy to accept seeming afflictions in His Name, and praise and worship Him with increased power while doing so. As one faces and accepts his problems and set-backs in this manner, even the most dire tragedies are transformed into blessings.

It may be that you are seeking some coveted public of- fice, or some high appointment, or have your heart set on some business advancement, only to find all your hopes tumbling into ruins around you. Not only may it appear that all your labors are lost but that your chances are for- ever shattered.

Or it may be the loss of a loved one has completely overwhelmed you with devastating despair. But remember this, when you grieve too long and too hard for the loss or departure of a beloved one, you are not mourning for them but for yourself. You are weeping over your own loss and loneliness and not for the departed one. They would not return if they could. And if you will think clearly, without considering your own viewpoint, neither would you recall them. If they are worthy of so great a love as yours, then you may be sure God esteems that worth and all is well!

It may be that your trusted partner failed you, he who had been a life-long friend. Yes, your loss or sorrow or difficulty could include any heartbreak or tragedy possible to imagine, for there is no adverse condition or seeming disaster that could not be included in this list of misfor- tunes. And everyone on the earth has faced one or more of them during his sojourn here in mortality. Some have even lived through all of them—and more! Along with every misfortune possible, their own lives have hung in the balance, while their worldly possessions were rent from their grasp and their very honor became besmirched and smeared with ridicule.

But if one's love is strong enough, he will be given the power to rise above the misfortunes, for he will be able to ride upon the storm. No matter what seeming disaster may strike, as it heaps up its distresses, suffering or humiliation, it can work together for one's good if he will work with it to fulfill the law and so prove his love. It is one's own vicissitudes that hold the power of his mastery. When one becomes the master of his own reactions to outside conditions, he may be sure he is very near to the kingdom of heaven.

Remember that Christ was crucified and in that crucifixion was exalted—and His labors also. And the very world itself was lifted into a higher state of existence.

In your own crucifixion and disappointments and seeming setbacks are held the stepping-stones of your own glorious progress and divine exaltation.

You may be thrown flat upon your face as it is ground down into the mud. You may be dishonored and reviled. You may be hungry and cold and in dire want, or worse; you may see your loved ones suffering from lack.

Your plans may all crumble into dust around you, but, in your hands and within your heart lies the power to turn the adverse conditions into good. If you keep your thoughts high and your vision "single to the glory of God" you will prove your love and the truth of His words will be established and fulfilled in you. You alone have the power to prove and fulfill them, that you might KNOW of their truth. And within you is the power to prove and fulfill His every promise.

If in your distresses and disappointments you accept His Divine Will as your only law, then His holy Will will begin to operate for your good. And for every loss there will be a greater gain, like Job of old, who received double for every loss, increased joy for every sorrow, higher honors for every humiliation.

In God's will is held only your own perfection. And as you learn the pure obedience, through your sufferings and disappointments, you will be enfolded in the glory of your own advancement and your own complete fulfilment. Then nothing that is adverse or evil will have the power to remain permanently against you. In this law all disasters are transmuted into blessings. Beyond the dismays and disappointments of misfortune is the power of transmutation. But you are the one who must put this ineffable power to use. You must *be-live* and so fulfill its promises.

"All things work together for good to them that love God."

Love, when fully expressed, holds no fears, no resentments, no self-pitying sorrow. Love holds within its divine essence the power to transmute or exalt any condition, regardless of what it is. And when one is filled with this exalted love, there is no evil that can stand in adversity against him. The evil is converted and transformed into good as its powers are utilized and turned into dynamic strength.

"All things work together for good to them that love God."

"All things" means every adverse condition, every loss,

every seeming tragedy or set-back, every failure and disappointment as well as every joy. As one proves his love by giving praise to God, instead of smoldering resentments and muttered condemnations, every condition will be worked out for a blessing to him for his own divine fulfilment. As one believes in the law, to the extent that he fulfills it, he soon learns of its unspeakable, dynamic powers. He KNOWS the truth of the promise and becomes free from the old bondage of misfortunes. His very knowledge of their truth is power unlimited.

"Gratitude" or the "great-attitude" holds the power of multiplication and of supply. Love itself fills one with the great gratitude as he gives silent thanks and praise in a devotion of melting, healing love. And that released gratitude, sent out on the wings of love, multiplies every blessing a hundred-fold; yea, more! It increases the little into plenty until there is not room enough to receive the supply. Man himself becomes the sacred cruse through which the oil of abundance is poured out.

Love is the transformer for it contains the complete power of transmutation. Love and gratitude and praise are the divine ingredients that transform all evils and misfortunes into joys and all sorrows into blessings. Love has the power to exalt every storm of adversity, every condition of dismay and every heart-rending tragedy into divine, eternal good. All sorrows and misfortunes can be lifted into beauty and be transformed into loveliness as man himself is exalted above the conditions by his own released love and gratitude.

In fulfilling the great love one is himself translated from a mediocre mortal into a being of power and vision and fulfilment. Against such no condition or force can stand in adversity. And all things work together for the good of him for he loves God so greatly there can be no bitterness nor resentments in him. And he becomes a son of Light, for "He who is thankful in all things shall be made glorious."

As only praise and thanks fill the soul, through the power of selective thinking, one becomes all that is wonderful and gracious and beautiful. Such a one fulfills the law of his own being and the higher law of divinity. Such a one is exalted from mortality and translated into a higher condition of existence—even immortality.

The law is your own to fulfill. And God bless you!

THE BIRTH OF THE SPIRIT

Chapter VIII

One is not born of the Spirit because he has espoused some religion or had certain ordinances performed over him and for him, as mankind has been taught to believe. These ordinances are beautiful and impressive and certainly not without merit but they are only the symbols of the true reality. They are often but the infant pacifiers of the searching soul.

The earthly ordinances are but the symbols used to gain admittance into some church that belongs to this earth. There is a higher church than any earthly organization. It is "The Church of the First Born" and consists of the great "Brotherhood of Light." This church belongs to a higher realm and in order to gain admittance into it one must go beyond the symbols and partake of their true reality. It is only the full *Truth* that can bring the fulfilment of so great a promise as that "spiritual birth."

One is born of the Spirit only when "The divine Light of Christ, which has been given to abide in every man who cometh into the world," is brought forth in its fulness. Only with the completion of this divine reality is one truly born of the Spirit. Then it is that one is so filled with Spirit he becomes Spiritual—or is Spirit. His physical being is exalted into a spiritual vibration mat is eternal and divine. In this new awareness and exalted condition the flesh and

71

all its weaknesses and desires are transformed and one becomes a new person—a literal son of God.

Within this birth of the Spirit is contained the dynamic
fulfilling glory of the released Christ Light as it fills the
individual with Its eternal Light and everlasting power.

As one *prepares himself,* through love and compassion
and inner devotion he grows into the vibration of Spirit
and Its boundless Light and eternal Truth become a very
part of him. One is only born of the Spirit when the great
Christ Light so fills his being It becomes a permanent factor.
When this happens it becomes as impossible for him to
return to the dark, mediocre level of mortal living and
thinking as it is for a chick to return to the egg, "Or for
a man to enter the second time into his mother's womb
to be born again."

It is only the TRUTH that will make one free—the
great Almighty Truth of God Himself and the unutterable
glory of His vibrating power of Eternal Light—or Spirit—
of Life. As one steps into the fulness of this Light, or
divine knowledge, he steps into a higher phase of existence.
This is not just a cherished membership in some church
organization. It is a spiritual birth that is a divine reality.
It is as literal as one's birth into mortality. And with this
birth of the Spirit one is admitted into membership with
the Church of the Firstborn, the Great Brotherhood of Light.

Christ, personally, does not redeem any man. Man is
redeemed as he brings forth that Christ Light contained
within himself. In that Light is his redemption held, and
Christ is its source. To bring forth that Light man must
learn to believe on His Name. And His Name is the great
Unspeakable Name of ineffable power. It is a Name that
is unspeakable because it is not contained within a word.

It is a Name that is held in the dynamic powers of an unutterable vibration—unutterable because it cannot possibly be spoken. No word or sounds can contain it. It is a vibration of exalting, limitless power. This unspeakable Name of promise cannot possibly be the spoken word of His Name, but the true reality of His Name as it is sent forth on His own vibration of Light in singing, triumphant, unutterable glory. This great Name, in which we are admonished to believe, cannot possibly be spoken in word—not in any language. His great ineffable Name, in which man is admonished to "believe" or "BE-LIVE", is the vibration of His holy Light as it is developed and brought forth from within through awareness expressed in tenderness and love.

To bring forth this great vibration of Christ Light is how one takes upon himself the Name of Jesus Christ, which the sacramental prayer designates. One takes upon himself the Christ vibration of Light and glory, even the Unspeakable Name when he develops that vibration within and brings forth Its everlasting Light of Eternal power. Celestial powers are released with the bringing forth of that holy Christ Light. As one is filled with this Light of Christ he is truly born of the Spirit even as the tiny pattern of an infant is fulfilled when that pattern is filled with flesh. Then it is born.

Those who bring forth this Light are actually doing the works which Christ did. And the greater works will follow.

The holy Light of Christ is but a small pilot Light lying dormant in the soul of man. One is only aware of it at first through that uneasy voice of conscience, or through that inner proclamation of divine approval that is bestowed through meritorious actions. This dim, flickering Light holds within It the divine Seed of God Himself. This Seed, that has been placed within the soul of every man is the "Holy, Immaculate Conception." It has been spoken of in awesome reverence down the centuries as the greatest mystery and belonging to Christ alone. None have comprehended that It belongs to every man. This precious, divine Seed is the very Seed of God Himself. And God implanted It in every man in the very beginning—even before the world was. It has always been man's to bring forth and to glorify. He who glorifies It and brings It forth will be glorified by It.

When one brings forth the Light of Christ until It fills his being permanently he is born of the Spirit. When he brings forth that divine Seed of God until it grows and matures to fill his entire being he receives "The Fulness of the Father," which is the greatest glory possible to receive.

As this great and holy calling, which belongs to every man, is *fulfilled,* that individual will be *filled-full* of the glory and the power of God. He will also be endowed with the divine power of Jesus Christ. He will arise from his dead, mortal estate into his divine maturity to receive and to fulfill all things. When this is achieved one is no longer a mere mortal. He takes on immortality. He "evolves from the man kingdom into the God Kingdom."

Man's mortal mind may exclaim in protest, "Impossible!" Then mortal man should let his doubting mind explain the transition of a crawling caterpillar into a flaming butterfly winging its way over the flower-spread beauty of earth.

Man has worked in reverse from the time when he first chose the difficult, mortal road. Man himself deliberately relinquished the divine way of God's choosing. He plunged himself into mortality and has been held steadfastly in its grasp ever since because of his lack of understanding. Yet always there has been the higher Way standing open for his return into the Paradisical realm of a more beautiful existence. That road is the "Straight and Narrow Road" that leads to immortality, without one needing to partake of death with its degrading, undignified sorrows and sufferings. That "Straight and Narrow Way" is the inner way. It is the Christ Way for it is through the Christ Light within that one must travel it. He who journeys along this road must bring forth that divine Christ Light and take upon himself that Unspeakable Name. Such a one is born of the Spirit and will *stand forth*—a new creature—even a son of God!

Man has worked entirely from the mortal, physical side of his nature. It is true that stupendous wonders have been conceived and brought forth by the powers of creatorship contained within the minds of men. Men are inherent creators by nature. But they have only used their powers to father a machine age of mechanical inventions because of their gross, blind ignorance. Man himself is as impotent as were his stone-age ancestors—even more so. No man of the present day has the ability to go forth alone into the wilderness and carve out a beautiful estate. He needs great machines to saw his lumber. He needs one man to make his bricks and another to lay them. He requires men and machines to cut his timbers. He probably needs help to swing his doors and to hang his windows. Knowledge is so concentrated and so specialized and so mechanically worked out that man has become only the weak, guiding robot of his own high-powered inventions.

Each year man himself has become less and less important, less secure, more unhappy and more and more impotent.

Man has literally dethroned himself and will assuredly destroy himself by the very power he has taken from himself to delegate to his machines unless he takes over the task of developing his own potentialities into the full measure of their divine purpose.

When man lifts his mind beyond the mechanical and financial and physical levels where he has placed it and begins to work upon himself and to explore his own potential powers he will begin to fulfill his own greatness. As he brings forth that holy Light of Christ from within himself, he will truly be born again. He will be born out of the physical, mortal estate into a higher spiritual realm of divine comprehension and existence. Then he will find himself to be far superior to anything he has created or achieved in his mechanical or political fields. He will stand awed and wonder-filled at the mighty, breathtaking glory of God's greatest handi-work—himself! Man is truly the greatest creation ever conceived, the most wonderful invention God ever fashioned, for within each and every man is an embryoed god, waiting for fulfilment. When man's divine potentialities begin to stir toward their quickening, man will arise from the dust and awake from the sleep of the ages! Man himself is the sacred instrument divine! He is the marvel and the wonder of existence. Man is the very expression of God when he fulfills the measure of his own creation. And assuredly, "All that the Father has is his!"

When this great quickening comes, and it will come whenever an individual begins to comprehend the powers and the super-faculties lying dormant within himself, he will be *fulfilled,* or *filled full* of the power and glory of God. This birth is the great actuality of being born again.

This is each individual's assignment as he releases the
Christ Light entombed within himself. This is a resurrection
as the divine Christ Light, long lying entombed within
each man, is released and brought forth. When this is accomplished, then will man's mechanical inventions rust
away and become as nothing. Man, in this new-found estate
will arise as a living part of the great Celestial vibration
of Light and will automatically move upward into his own
divine perfection, crowned with infinite glory and eternal
power—a son of Light.

Man has worked backward from the beginning. He has
yearned and striven for power, not to govern and control
himself, but to govern and control others. Most men, when
given any power or authority use it to strip all other men
of like power. They seek to bring all men into subjection
to themselves. These usurpers of free-agency desire greatly
to enslave the minds of men as they enforce their own wills
and their ideas and methods upon the lives of their fellowmen. This is the same power Lucifer always exerts over
his subjects.

Man has desired power to perform miracles, while he
has persistently concealed and denied the miracle of eternity
contained right within himself. He has yearned to be en-
throned upon the pinnacle of the temple that he might awe
the minds of men and prove that he alone is endowed with
the super-powers of divinity. And in such desiring, his
thoughts have turned to the little, mortal, physical "self"
as he has blocked his own way to progress.

In all selfish desiring, man has but locked his own divinity more securely within his heart and reinforced that
seal upon the great stone slab guarding its tomb. Man,
with these personal desires held uppermost in his mind,

is but a small child. He is but a third grade student yearning for the credits of a college degree without first mastering fully the mystery of the alphabet.

In man's yearning to perform miracles, he has been unwilling to prepare himself so that he could become worthy of so great a work. He has sought to change everything but himself, and everyone but himself. Man has made no effort to purify the inside of himself, as he has conformed to the outside cleansing methods expounded by mortal ritualists. Man has made no effort to train himself to even believe or to *Be* and *Live* according to those great inner teachings—or to believe even in His Name—His great Unspeakable Name—the Name of ineffable, fulfilling power and Light, or to take upon himself that Name or vibration. Neither has man made any effort to hold himself within those holy vibrations of Light by his own exalted thinking habits.

When any man brings forth that divine Light, or vibration, that is unspeakable in its power, It will go forth to do the works. Man will then know that the power to move mountains, to raise the dead, to heal the deaf, the blind and the lame is contained within that holy vibration of Light as It is sent forth on the wings of love. He will know that even the power to feed the thousands—or the whole world, for that matter, as well as himself and his loved ones, is contained within that Light.

When man realizes that, "Of his little mortal self he can do nothing," perform no miracles, do no great works, and accomplish no permanent good, he will let go of his own impotencies and let that Light of Christ Vibration come forth until It fills his entire being as it flows on out to help heal and glorify a world. He will be like an electric light bulb that receives the full power of the current and *stands forth* to light up the world—his own world. Then it is that he will be born of the Spirit and take on immortality.

The bringing forth of the great Light is the major work which Jesus accomplished. All other works are predicated upon this one master achievement. And this is the work He left in our hands. This is the assignment that has been waiting down the centuries for us to fulfill, that we might step forth into our own divinity and become "co-heirs with Him", not just in words and beautifully worded phrases, not in shouted fanaticism—but in actual power.

One is born of the Spirit when he brings forth the Christ Light from within until it fills his being. Then it is that he grows into Its fulness and is born of the Spirit. Everything else is only the symbol of this divine reality.

When one comprehends the great Christ Light, he will understand the powers contained in that dynamic vibration of glory and will be lifted into a new dimension of comprehension, a new world of profound, indescribable glory. Christ's Light and the vibration of His Unspeakable Name are but the stupendous vibration of one's fulfilment when it is brought forth in its fulness.

The higher vibration of Light and fulfilment can only be contacted and brought forth through the wondrous law of love. Love casts out all fear. It dissipates all negative thoughts and conditions. Love is a singing glory that fulfills all other laws and gathers all divine vibrations into a concentrated power of completion.

Those who learn to hold themselves in the Light of Christ, as it is brought forth from within by their own efforts, learn to think on a higher level. As they continually lift their thoughts to new and higher visions, they soon receive a fulness of that divine Light. These enlightened ones will act from inspired impulses that turn into complete knowledge and power. These advancing ones are filled with gratitude and love for the new understanding and as their appreciation grows they advance speedily until that Light takes over and begins to direct and glorify their lives. And then it is that they comprehend all things. These noble ones will enter the realm where all things become comprehensible and therefore possible.

It is impossible for a tiny child to make a cake. It is a simple task for one who has all the "know how" and the ingredients.

These enlightened ones, with the *"spiritual* know-how," naturally step through into a higher dimension to join the "Great Brotherhood of Light," known as the "Church of the Firstborn," or "The Church of Enoch."

These titles must be made clear, for they do not pertain to any earthly organization. The Brotherhood of Light consists of those who have brought forth that divine Light of Christ from within themselves until they are filled with It and so are born into a higher vibration of existence. This great organization is also known as "The Church of the Firstborn." This title designates those who have been born into the Spirit, literally, during their earthly experience. They achieved the stupendous accomplishment of being born into the great Spiritual Light or vibration without having to enter the other realm through death. Not too many have accomplished this wonderful thing. This glorious Church is also known as "The Church of Enoch," because Enoch was the first mortal to make that transition from mortality into immortality without tasting death or partaking of it. This group is composed of the choice ones of the ages—those who have *overcome, while in the flesh.*

There are many of the present generation who are being prepared speedily for this wonderful transition. These dynamic, progressive, enlightened ones will soon be prepared to step through into that higher dimension, though it is to be an individual accomplishment for each one. As they step through they will automatically be born of the water. This wonderful experience will be fully revealed in the following chapter. And those who are born of the water and of the Spirit have the power to overcome death.

You great and wondrous ones, arise! And take upon you His Name—His great Unspeakable Name and clothe yourselves in Its Light.

"And I put off darkness and clothed myself with light, and my soul acquired a body free from sorrow, or affliction or pain." And again: "I have put on incorruption through His Name; and have put off corruption by His grace. Death hath been destroyed before my face; and Sheol hath been abolished by my word; And there hath gone up deathless life in the Lord's land, and hath been made known to His faithful ones, and hath been given without stint to those that trust in Him." (Odes of Solomon).

Beloved, such is your heritage! And such can be your fulfilment.

THE RIVER OF LIFE

Chapter IX

Now I must speak of the sacred reality of being born of the water, of which the earthly ordinance of baptism is but the symbol.

Between the two realms, the lower and the higher, is the River of Life. The higher realm extends upward into infinitude, glory ascending above and beyond glory. The lower realm includes this world and everything that is beneath it. It descends into the lowest realms of the bottomless and embraces the outer realms of darkness.

Between these two realms, that meet together on the borderland of earth and the higher dimension, there is the River of Life. Its waters are more real and sparkling and alive than any singing mountain river. It pulsates with joy and vibrates with a sheer, exquisite beauty that is impossible to describe. Sunlight sparkling on diamonds is the best description that can be given.

The waters of the most frolicking streams on earth, can and do often come to a stale "dead end" slough of stagnancy and defilement. They can end in a contaminated swamp that breeds disease and pestilence. However, the waters of that bounteous River of Life can never be restricted, retarded nor defined.

This River can best be described by using some of earth's scientific knowledge as comparisons. The whole world is completely enfolded in the ethers and oxygens and the various elements and substances which make up the air we breathe. And though the entire earth is completely enfolded and surrounded in this refined substance we call "air" nevertheless there are certain air currents and trade winds which are like living streams or rivers. They flow forth in their destined channels as they continually renew and give life to the whole encompassing atmosphere—and to the world.

There are the great and mighty oceans of water, vast and extensive, covering the larger portion of the earth's surface. And through and across these vast bodies of water there are also currents and streams that are like great, stupendous rivers, flowing onward forever and forever, renewing and revitalizing the whole.

The energy and power used to keep these vast streams circulating can never be computed by the minds nor be measured with the instruments of man. The manpower or the kilowats used in operating a small pump can give only the faintest idea of the exerted energy used to keep those ocean currents flowing onward—ever onward. These vast currents are miles wide and their depth has not been measured as they encircle the earth in their endless journey of revitalization.

There is the Gulf Stream of the Atlantic, bringing its warming, beneficial balm and blessings to many shores and many lands. There is the Japanese Current of the Pacific, with its like powers of functioning. There is the Labrador Current. And there are numerous smaller currents and tributaries, which lend their life-giving vitality to keep alive the whole, vast, stupendous seas. It is not necessary to name or number them all here.

It is only necessary for one to stop for a moment to contemplate the majesty of such mighty rivers, flowing through the oceans as they hold the power of life, of warmth and of renewal in their everlasting tides, in order to comprehend the fullness of this explanation. If one, in that brief moment of contemplation, will let the breath of joyous wonder enter his being as he stands in awe at the wisdom and power so profound that it can create and hold these tides in control, he will, in that moment, be very close to the Truth. The reverent awe these thoughts awaken is "The fear of the Lord," expressed of old.

When contemplated thus, the existence of every created thing becomes a revealed miracle of unfathomable magnitude.

Now, to return to the River of Life. When ministers speak of "the other side," they are referring to or designating the life on the other side of that River—the life beyond mortality—the life beyond death. In a way this is correct, but in another way it is quite erroneous. "The other side" need not refer to death at all. Many die who do not have the power nor the privilege of crossing that River of Life. These unhappy, disembodied ones remain on *this* side of that River completely unaware that it even exists. And because of their unworthiness they are deprived of its power and beauty and glorifying, perfecting potentialities.

The River of Life could be likened to the ocean currents in this way: every existing thing which God has created is enfolded or immersed in His great and wondrous love—a love that fills all time and all space. It is everywhere. Man is always enfolded in the unspeakable power of this boundless love. Man has either taken this love for granted, ignored it, rejected it, denied it, or through his ignorance, remained unaware of it and its life-giving strength and purifying glory.

Nevertheless the love is always there, always awaiting man's acceptance of it. "Abide in me and I will abide in you." "Turn unto me and I will turn unto you," are God's own eternal promises given unto men.

Now, to describe the River and reveal its purpose and meaning and its powers. Flowing through the vast glory of God's enfolding love is also a current or stream. It is a River of God's concentrated love, intensified and magnified a thousand-fold. This concentrated stream of God's intensified love is the *River of Life*. Because these mighty waters are the concentrated love of God, they hold the power of renewal and of cleansing and of restoration for any individual who prepares himself to pass through them. To be prepared to enter these holy waters, one must begin to develop the gift of love.

The powers contained within the Waters of Life are almost incomprehensible. These waters contain the divine, wondrous power to wash away the very *effects* and *results* of one's errors and his sins and mistakes. The sins and weaknesses are consumed through the bringing forth of the divine Christ Light. In the releasing of this glorious Light the mortal transgressions are forgiven, the weakness consumed and the sins overcome. But even then the results of those weaknesses and transgressions and sins remain with all their lingering hurts and effects until one is immersed in the great purifying River of Life and receives that divine birth of the water in its true reality.

As one learns to hold forth his sins and weaknesses and transgressions in that redeeming flame of Christ's holy

Light they are consumed by His glory and one is free. Then it is that he is prepared to receive the life more abundant—even Life Eternal, which Christ so definitely promised. This ancient promise is fulfilled unto one as he goes down into the waters of the great River of Life and is literally born of the Waters as he comes up out of them.

This birth, or baptism contains the great healing and the full glorifying, restoring power of all perfection. All things are made perfect and are exalted by it. All conditions are transformed and readjusted and are completely transmuted into the perfect plan God held in His mind in the beginning of creation. There is only one condition which man has to fulfill, he has to be willing as he makes every effort within his powers to receive these complete blessings of God's boundless, transforming love.

As one yields up his sins and his weaknesses he becomes a new person. As he humbly, penitently yields up the *effects* and *results* of his errors and mistakes and sins into the healing, restoring power of Almighty God's boundless River of concentrated love, the scars and hurts and often terrifying results of his blundering, whether ignorantly or intentionally performed, can be healed. Even the wounds he may have inflicted upon the hearts and minds of his loved ones and his friends and associates as well as those inflicted purposely upon those whom he considered his enemies, can be restored to the perfection of God's infinite, loving power of complete sanctification.

This is the great healing that must come. This is the healing Christ promised. This is the healing that is beyond anything physical man has ever dreamed of, or even longed for. In this great and glorious healing the *effects* and *results* of all one's errors and sins and weaknesses are washed out

into the great ocean of God's creative power and are transformed and transmuted as they are adjusted to conform to
His divine and holy plan. The dynamic powers of God
are the powers of creation. The powers of His forgiving
love, as one partakes of it, through obedience, contains
also the power of "un-doing" all the evils one may have
wrought during his blind, arrogant living, or by his great
ignorance or deliberate rebellion.

It must be here remembered that in God's plan is held
all the perfection, the splendor and the honor and glory
possible for one to receive.

Within the Light or vibration of Christ is contained the
power of redemption and forgiveness and overcoming.
Within the River of Life is contained the power of sanctification and of perfection so that even the effects of one's
sins are blotted out.

Man, in his mortal blindness, has continually fought
against the Will of God. He has not realized that within
the Will of God all joys and gifts and blessings are held
in all their divine abundance and overflowing, breathtaking perfection—blessings and gifts so far beyond anything
mortal man is capable of comprehending or conceiving,
he would be utterly blinded by their brilliance if he glimpsed
them, even partially, before his own purification was accomplished. "Eye hath not seen, nor ear heard, neither
hath it entered into the heart of man, the things God hath
prepared for them that love him."

These dynamic, breathtaking blessings are not intended
for only a few. These blessings are intended for each and
every individual who will learn to place himself in tune
with the Will of God, for obedience is true love in its
fullest expression.

As one learns to hold himself in the fountain of God's almighty love he lets go of the little, mortal "self" and it is dissolved and the great, dynamic, Christ-enlightened soul of himself steps forth to fill the place of a redeemed, sanctified son of God.

Also within the waters of the beautiful River of Life is contained the power of the great healing that will eventually heal and restore the earth and every living soul who will accept of Its blessings and prepare himself to receive them. Within these sacred waters is held the power to heal even the memory of one's errors and mistakes and sins so that "they will never come into remembrance before the Lord." They will also be erased from the memory of the individual who committed them and from the memories of those who may have been injured by those misdeeds of rebellion, defiance or ignorance or deliberate wickedness.

The thing required to participate in these wondrous blessings is that one begin to develop the gift of love. The waters of the River of Life are the concentrated, outflowing powers of God's love and only by bringing forth some degree of that love from within one's own heart is it possible to share in the healing wonders of its divine properties and powers.

And it is only through these dynamic waters of love that one can possibly step across into the higher realm of divine activity and progress and exaltation.

Anyone returning from the other side to render service to this earth must do so by again going down through those waters in order to be completely fortified for his assigned task. This is necessary in order for one to endure the dark,

discordant, evil vibrations of a world so engulfed in sin
and selfishness and greed as this earth is.

This great stream of Life was comprehended in a small
way by all the ancient peoples of the earth. The Hebrews
designated it as their own River Jordan, using the physical symbol of their own stream and their own entrance
into the "promised Land" as a pattern to express the crossing of that River of Life into the realms of heaven.

This sacred River of Life has stood between the two
worlds from the very beginning. It is the eternal dividing
line between those who remain in their discords, their
dislikes and their hates and those who develop the gift of
love. Those who love much, automatically develop and
bring forth the Christ Light. When the impulse of Love's
compassionate, tender forgiveness are developed until they
transcend every other impulse and vibration, one will have
the power to fulfill all things.

This love is the love that must be rendered to God with
all one's heart, all his mind, and all his soul and all his
strength. It is the love that must reach out to enfold not
only one's own, but his neighbors and acquaintances—and
his enemies—and then go forth to encompass the world in
the warmth of its redeeming, forgiving tenderness.

Thus it is that *all the laws are fulfilled* by those who
live in perfect accord with those first two Great Commandments. Those who fulfill this law of divine love and
obedience will be born of the water and of the Spirit in
very truth, which reality so far surpasses any mortal symbols there is no comparison.

"So, beloved, let us love one another; for love is of God;
and everyone that loveth is born of God, and knoweth
God. He that loveth not knoweth not God; for God is

'love." (I John 4:7-8). This love cannot be feigned. It must be real as it comes forth from the depths of one's heart, flowing out to bless and heal a world. This love can only be achieved or obtained through earnest prayer for it is required that one "pray for this pure Christ-like love with all the energy of heart."

As one seeks for this love it will begin to flow to him and at last it will enfold and glorify him as it flows henceforth out through his own open heart. "This is the Fruit of the Tree of Life, the love of God that is shed forth through the hearts of the children of men."

The ancient Egyptians often depicted their departed sailing forth in boats as they drew their elaborate pictures on the walls of their temples and tombs. To the Egyptians, the painted pictures of boats served the purpose of literal boats, for, after all, the journey was a spiritual one. Nevertheless, because of ignorance, the individual's physical belongings and treasures, along with all necessary equipment, including a servant or two and perhaps his wife, were sealed in the tomb to take that journey with him.

In the Egyptian Book of the Dead the River of Life is frequently referred to.

The ancient Grecians had a vivid awareness of the River of Life, though to them it came to represent more the river of death than the exalted River of Life. In their mythology the ferryman, who bore the newly arrived dead across the "Styx" or River, was named "Charon." Even in this negative belief they acknowledged man's survival of the change called *death*. Their negative idea of the River did not develop until they, as a people, degenerated and transgressed the laws of their own natures and inborn ethics.

In the beginning the word "Charon" meant literally, "One who guides," or "One who conducts." Charon was a title of honor or appointment, not a personal name. Charon was the title of anyone who was sent to escort others across that great, wondrous River. In time, because of increasing wickedness and hence growing superstition, with its consequent fears and engendered ignorance, Charon began to represent one grewsome individual who eventually became a black-robed, sinister figure armed with a scythe—"the angel of death."

No *one* individual has ever been assigned the responsibility of assisting others across that sacred stream, yet none ever cross it for the first time unescorted. Only in love can that River be crossed and only those who love greatly are sent to guide loved ones or friends—or others, according to the divine assignment, through those holy Waters of Life.

To the various Indian tribes of America, the River of Life was quite real. There were a few tribes who buried their dead, not in graves, but in pure, running water. They too sent a man's belongings, and often a horse, along with him to carry him safely across the stretches of "no-man's-land" before he embarked upon the great shining waters. They believed the great oceans were literally those shining waters of Life, which they called "The Many Waters." When the white man and the Spaniards came from across the seas the Indians welcomed them as gods, thinking they had come from heaven, or their Happy Hunting Ground.

The Hindoos likewise knew of the River and consecrated the Ganges to stand as a symbol of it on this earth. Their pilgrimages to this muddy, polluted stream, as they plunge themselves into it, believing it will purify and sanctify them, is well known. And, until the British government ended the practice, a man's wife was burned with him on his funeral pyre—and the very pyre itself was intended to represent a boat.

The Norsemen knew of the great River of Life and instead of burying their heroes they set their bodies adrift on burning boats or barges, believing that by the time the boat had finished burning the individual would have arrived at the far shore of the River and be welcomed into Valhalla by Odim himself.

The ancient Persians, under Zoroaster, knew of the reality of the mighty River of Life and they both sang and wrote of it.

The Sarawak Caverns on the Island of Borneo, which have recently been re-discovered, are filled with boat caskets hewn from hollowed-out logs. Many of these boat coffins still contain the bones of their dead.

Every ancient race and people had a knowledge of this sacred River of Life, which in time became garbled by tradition and through their oft repeated legends. However there is no need to mention and name all the races and peoples and tribes who stood in reverent awe at the very thought of that River, nor to go further into detail concerning their separate beliefs which tell the same story in their own, often distorted, ways.

Poets from time immemorial have sung of the beauties of that River. Christian churches have chanted of its glory in their hymns and anthems while the records of all the ancient races of the earth have testified to its reality.

On "the other side" of that wondrous River one is lifted into an entirely new and higher vibration of life that is difficult to describe. I can only share with you its beauty and purpose and reality as you are willing and able to lift your vision beyond the tangible things your physical eyes are able to behold.

Light is measured by degree and understanding is measured by Light which continually increases as one goes onward into the higher realms. There is no limit to which an advancing, love-filled individual may ascend as he becomes increasingly aware of his surroundings. As he advances, new and higher vistas of progress and unutterable beauty unfold. It is a realm of ever increasing joy and power and continued achievement.

The distance between you and that holy River of Life can only be measured by your own awakening awareness or consciousness. Sometimes it takes centuries to journey from this world to that River. And there are those who never make it. It is a journey, not of distance, but of mental and spiritual awakening. Each makes that journey according to his or her unfolding vision and according to his own individual desiring and degree of love. Advancement comes with increasing knowledge and faith and love and with expanding spiritual vision, one brings forth that divine Light of Christ right within himself and so develops the gift of love. The Light of understanding and the love of outpouring unselfishness must both be developed in order for one to cross that River of Love.

Love itself requires nurturing and willing and letting and continual growth. No one can transform himself from a *"hateful"* person into a loving one in an instant—or a day. In the realm of glory, love must become the eternal reality of one's being, not just a shallow, mooded emotion hung on a weathervane. Neither can it be incipid, weak or feigned. It is impossible to counterfeit love and try to use the counterfeit as the golden coin of admission into the higher dimensions. Real love has to become the all-encompassing part of one's entire nature. It must become a very part of the individual in its unfailing, joyous, exquisite beauty and power as it carries forth the Light. Such love is beyond all substitutes and all imagining. And one must actually become that love.

No one is able to even approach, let alone cross the great River of Life, who is not spiritually prepared, *whether in mortality—or out of it*. This is not because the River and its divine properties are forbidden. It is simply "out of bounds" because those who will not accept God's love cannot possibly comprehend it. Nor could they endure the enfolding, glorifying essence of that powerful baptism if they are not prepared to receive it.

All those who are worthy to be born of the water and partake of its glory, receive the power to send out the vibrations of that increased love in some measure. Those who do not love God, or their fellowmen, are not yet qualified to comprehend His great healing, perfecting, wondrous love, nor can they receive of its boundless blessings.

To partake of the great love one must learn to bestow love in a selfless, outpouring benediction of silent com-. passion. In this service one is required to love more than just his own near and dear ones—and those who love him. He is required to develop this love until it can enfold his neighbors and then, reaching out, gather the whole human race in its tenderness. It must enfold one's enemies until they too are healed of their dislikes and their hates and their evils.

As love flows out from an individual, the greater love pours into him in an ever increasing degree. Love must flow. It must never become stagnant. Love cannot be taken for granted. Neither is it enough that one be a sweet-tempered individual, free from discords and dislikes. One must develop love until it becomes an actual, living power as it flows out from him in its course of blessing and of healing. When these currents of love are released from within an individual, he is truly partaking of the fountains of living water and they are flowing forth from his heart in their benediction of silent, powerful glory.

God's great love has never been withheld from any child of His divine creating. God's love enfolds the world and makes alive all things. When His children open up their hearts to this love and permit it to flow through their beings, they will not only be purified and cleansed by its dynamic power of exquisite beauty, they will be completely healed by it. They will then have the power to send that love out to enfold whomsoever they desire to assist, or to any in need. It has no limits when magnified and sent out through an open, understanding heart. This love is known in the higher realms as "The Love of God Substance." It can be used at all times for the benefit of man—and for his healing.

To those who first view that mighty River of Life it appears to be of the substance and consistency of water in its clearest most beautiful degree. To those who have advanced into the higher life it is soon comprehended to be composed of the concentrated life-force of God's almighty, dynamic love, which is spiritual. This love is the creative and the sustaining and the renewing power of the universe from the atom upward.

This River is literally the point of egress as one steps

beyond the vibrations and influences of the earth. It is not a river one rows across, as some have believed. Neither is it a stream one can swim across. It is *"entered into"* and one *"comes up out of it."*

This River is entirely spiritual in its sublime essence, for it is love. And blessed are those who are prepared to pass through it for it is Life. In going down into its waters and crossing through them, by being completely immersed in it, one does not need to hold his breath, nor need to be afraid. This River IS *Life*—and the breath of Life is contained in it.

As one learns to hold himself in the fountain of God's Almighty love, he lets go of the little ego-filled self. It is dissolved and the sanctified soul of himself steps forth to fulfill its glorified destiny. This ultimate perfection, this fulness of joy and happiness and every conceivable good, has always been the plan. Down the milleniums it has been awaiting man's acceptance of it. In God's will there is nothing but the divine, triumphant, beautiful fulfilment of every man's own inborn greatness. It is in God's Will that all joy, all happiness and all perfection are held.

One need not die in order to hold himself in the healing properties of that great River of Life. That River has always existed—will always exist. Man has only to alert his soul to comprehend.

The true reality is that each and every individual who will but prepare himself to believe, or *be* and *live* according to the divine law and love of his own being, will be given the power to hold himself within the cleansing, life-giving waters of that sacred, holy River of Life. This experience is an actual reality, not just a mortal symbol.

The sacred privilege of being immersed in the River of Life, as stated previously, *transmutes or eliminates the effects of every regretted error and mistake.* Not only the present is perfected through this divine experience but the past also. All things are healed and beautified by the tender power of God's Almighty love as one aligns himself with it.

THE FLAME-SHOD ONES

Chapter X

Upon arising, if one will but immerse himself within that holy, life-renewing stream of God's almighty love, holding himself in it for a few moments as he consciously partakes of its gifts and blessings, he will walk forth into the day, flame-shod and clothed in Light.

If each night, he again holds himself within the hallowed, renewing power of that River of Love he will be cleansed of all the earthly vibrations that have accumulated during the day. By so doing he can be renewed and invigorated as he receives the "life more abundant—even *Life Eternal!*"

It is as simple a proceeding for one in the flesh to enter into the waters of that holy River as it is for one who has gone through that change called "death." The great life-giving River is always there for man's benefit, only man has not been aware of it. In the spiritual realm there is neither time nor space. This statement is difficult for man to correlate into fact. The comprehension of this eternal truth is more a condition of expanded awareness and understanding than of departure and of travel and arrival.

Since an understanding of the River of Life is a state of comprehension, it must be made more apparent through a simple explanation. It must first be explored by the mind, as the soul lends its faculties of discernment and of belief.

It is impossible to comprehend the spiritual realm by any of the mere physical senses. The mind is the instrument of faith when properly trained and used. Therefore, it is the mind that must be exerted to explore the realms beyond the dominion of the five inferior, mortal senses. When the mind is used, instead of one's physical equipment, one begins to work with the dynamic principle of faith and so prepares himself to enter the realm of power.

The mind itself is marvelous beyond ordinary thought. The mind is fluid. It has faculties and powers of which man has never dreamed. It does not need to travel in order to *arrive*. The mind can instantly be at any spot on the earth and linger in any period of time. It can explore the universe. It can focus itself within an atom and examine its component parts. It can reach out to contemplate the vastness of eternity. It has only to open up to an awareness or consciousness of any far-flung realm or place in order to be there.

The mind can venture into a small boy's pocket or a human heart. It can explore the feathery substance of a cloud. It can soar along the Milky Way. It can ride upon a sunbeam or be instantly on the remotest start. It can mentally contemplate the surface of the moon and again return. It can visit any period of time or stand again in any remembered place of the past. The mind can reach into the realms of love and send that same love forth, increased and beautified, to heal and bless as one worships and adores.

Man's present desolate estate has been the result of his failure to develop and use the unlimited powers of his mind—and of his heart.

It has been said that "a democratic country is a country

in which people can say what they think—without think-ing." If mankind ever begins to understand its own ca-pacity to think it will begin to develop speedily along the dynamic roads of progress that have remained unexplored and outside of man's ken. Mind is the instrument which must be used in order to enter the realms of faith. This realm of faith is the realm of things and conditions that is now considered *the impossible!* It is impossible only be-cause man has not opened his spiritual eyes to see and his spiritual ears to hear and his soul to permit understanding and Light to come forth. The only thing that has been almost impossible has been man himself.

As one learns to *be* and *live* according to his highest knowledge and to reach for things beyond the touch of his physical hands, he will soon learn how simple a thing it is for him to immerse himself in the sacred waters of God's great River of Love. He will learn of its potent, un-limited powers and will realize that in this divine River is the true baptism of purifying forgiveness. He will know that this is the true reality behind all earthly ordinances and rituals and mortal symbols.

It is a simple thing for one who has opened up his mind to fathom and to use his own limitless capacity of thought, to comprehend the reality and wonder of God's great, boundless love which eternally surrounds him. Then, as he learns to rejoice in the breathtaking power and the healing properties of that love, he will have the power to bring the full, complete, flowing current of that mighty River of Life right to himself. One does not need to travel to that River. ONE DOES NOT NEED TO DIE IN ORDER TO REACH IT! That River comes to the individual whenever he is prepared and ready for so great and holy an ordinance.

One will be immersed in that holy River of Life as he opens up his heart, mind and soul to the great, living vibrating love and lets it flow through his own being to enfold the world. This is the healing that must come. And it will come first to the one who sends that love forth. Then it will heal those whom he enfolds in it.

As man increases and multiplies the powers of love in this manner, that love will eventually bring its divine healing to the whole world. This love must first be sent through the open hearts of the children of men, for out of men's hearts must flow the "Fountains of Living Waters!" And no one can approach that River or draw it to himself and receive of its almost incomprehensible blessings, who does not love greatly. Those who hate and who have developed only hateful feelings and release criticizing thoughts, can never approach that divine River of Love, let alone cross it.

One must relinquish every hate-filled (hateful) thought, every antagonistic, discordant, evil vibration; every feeling of resentment and jealousy. He must let go of his greeds and his fears and his lusts.

To even begin to contemplate that River mentally, one must first cast out his doubts and his negative thoughts and standardized ideas. He must begin to enter the mental realm where faith is the dynamic condition of supreme power. One must learn to control his disbelieving habits and in doing so conquer his "unbelief." This is what was anciently known as "exercising great and mighty faith." This exercise of faith is within everyone's power. And it is every man's privilege to make use of it. It is most necessary that those who refuse to remain mentally and spiritually retarded and undeveloped, begin this simple exercise. It is as necessary to exercise faith as it is to exercise one's physical body, in order that he does not remain a flabby-minded individual, ruled by his own doubts.

To become powerful in mind and soul and actions, one must commence to *be-lieve*, which is done merely by the simple process of being and living according to the greater, dynamic truths, truths which his physical eyes have not yet beheld nor his physical, mortal senses analyzed. He must explore with his mental faculties as he courageously steps forth into new, unexperienced adventures.

As one begins to live according to the greater teachings, he will soon KNOW the divine truth of them. This is the promise given to all men. It cannot fail! To *believe* one has only to *be live,* or to live and think according to the holy promises given to the children of men. Believing is a thing of action and of expression and of power. It is a way of life that develops knowledge and "KNOWLEDGE IS POWER!"

As one opens up his heart, soul and mind wide to that holy, stupendous, healing vibration of love and permits it to pour out through his own heart, it will begin its healing work, first within the individual, then it will go out to enfold his loved ones, his friends, his associates and then go on to encompass the world in its benediction as it blesses all.

Only in divine, purified, selfless love, can the River of Life be approached. It must be a sincere love, clothed in humility. And, only by man's releasing that love can he possibly partake of the fulness of love's renewing, anointing, purifying glory. Selfless love must fill the heart of him who would enter the holy River of God for the River is Love—and *It is Life!* And those who enter into it become flame-shod, in that their feet can never again be soiled by the unholy vibrations of earth.

Love is the great life-giving force of Creation. It is the power behind the "Life more Abundant!" It contains the greatest healing force in all existence. It is the reality behind creation. It is the very foundations upon which the earth was built and the universe laid. It holds the power of man's sanctification. It contains the perfection of all existence and the complete redemption and divine exaltation of man.

This River of Life is spiritual in its essence, even as pure love is spiritual. No human eyes have ever gazed upon pure love. No mortal hands have ever touched the everlasting texture of its effulgent splendor. No mere physical senses of man have power to reveal its etherial substance of unutterable, eternal beauty. No individual has heard with his physical ears, the full harmonious tones of its sublime symphony, unless he has been completely embued within those waters. Nevertheless, love is not a myth simply because it has not been weighed and measured and photographed with mechanical devices, nor looked at through a magnifying glass. No human eyes have been developed to see so refined an element. Mortal vision beholds only the tangible things of this grubby, physical world. It is impossible for one to hold love in the palm of his hand. Love only abides where love is. Love multiplies in him who sends it out. Love is a spiritual essence, an influence, a dynamic, indestructible power, which must be held within the heart of man.

Only those who have sinned greatly, deny love and this is so because they have so hardened their hearts through hate and transgression, they have sealed themselves out from it and have sealed it out from themselves. They may have been so unfortunate as to never have known its rapturous glory, or else to have forgotten its sublime, exquisite tenderness.

Every child should become acquainted with love, in his earliest childhood. It is every child's natural heritage. Infants are most susceptible to love. Under the right environment a child should grow into it, as it becomes established within his newly acquired mortal body. It is a sad fact to state that most children have it driven or beaten out of them almost from infancy, instead of being trained within its warmth, as they develop and mature within the sacred, holy security of love.

And again, lest there be those whose understandings have become defiled and polluted by immoral lust-filled thoughts and acts, I must state that love does not mean "sex". Sex is a physical instinct, shared alike by beast and reptile and insect and worm. The sex impulse is the animal instinct. Love is. the most exalted, sublime power in existence. Love is of God.

The River of Life is as real and as dynamic as the power and the reality of love, for it is concentrated love in all its healing radiance. As one permits his thoughts to expand and his mental powers to contemplate the things of the spirit, he will become spiritualized and his vision will begin to encompass the marvels of eternity. His hands begin to carry the power of eternal blessings in their touch and his feet become flame-shod, as they tread in understanding upon the upward path of glory.

As one learns to hold himself within the sacred waters of that divine River of Life, the powers of glory and truth will fill his entire being and the currents of the exalted love will open up new and mighty channels right within his own being, as its forces become apparent in the individual's life and so will they become forever established unto him. As this divine force of healing and perfection flows out through one's own being, he will comprehend that this is "The love of God that must be shed forth through the hearts of the children of men," that the great healing might come to individuals, to nations and to the world. He will leran also that these waters of God's Love, as they are shed through the heart of himself are truly "The Fruits of the Tree of Life!"

As one learns to immerse himself in this River and so becomes an open channel through which the love of God flows forth, he becomes an esetablished fountain for the living waters of life. He will also become renewed in body, mind and soul and henceforth will obtain the gift of "The life more abundant, even of Life Eternal!" His feet will become flame-shod as he steps forth into higher vibrations and service among the exalted ones—the noble Brotherhood of Light.

As one prepares himself and learns to hold himself within the mighty, healing current of that Holy River of Life, he partakes of Life Eternal. And, thereafter, death will have no claim upon him. "He will have the power to overcome the last enemy—even death!"

These are the waters Christ spoke of when he conversed with the Samaritan woman at the well. These are the waters He promised in which "A man need never thirst again!" These are the waters which will open a man's being so that "out of his heart will flow fountains, or rivers of living water!"

Man first explored the material world as he journeyed over its surface using his physical senses in his conquests. Then the realm of matter and its component parts, from the atom to the far flung stars and planets of the heavens, opened before his challenging mind. He has used his abilities and intelligence to measure and classify physical substance and the visible realms as he has pushed back the barriers of the unknown.

It is now time for man to begin the greatest search of all—the search for his own soul. With all his toiling and all his conquests he has failed to gain understanding. He has ignored the challenge of the Sermon on the Mount. He has made no effort to find out what it will do for him. He has failed to love his enemies but has increased his hates. He has made no great endeavor to love God with *all* his heart, with *all* his mind and with *all* his soul. His thoughts have only turned to God, as a rule, in extreme emergencies and then with either a groveling petitioning or a rebellious defiance. Man has completely failed to find out what great, unspeakable powers are held in the divine essence and gift of love. Nor has man awakened to the stupendous use of faith, when it is *exercised*. And never has man used the power of his mind to explore the spiritual realm—that divine reality of his own soul. And for this reason man himself is still floundering in complete impotency, a victim of disease, old age, misfortunes—and death.

He who will immerse himself in the River of Life, while in mortality, will find all barriers dissolved before him. Then it will be his privilege to immerse himself in that River of Life as often as he desires until he becomes the very love that stream of Life embraces. It is possible for one to so exalt himself in that Christ Light and in those

holy Waters of Life, he actually becomes love and light
as he steps forth flame-shod into the realms of glory.

As one continues to enter that sacred stream, he will
soon comprehend its purest essence and its divine properties, until he becomes the Master of them. It is then that
"all things become subjected unto him, both in heaven and
on earth; the Light and the Life; the Spirit and the power,
sent forth by the will of the Father, through Jesus Christ,
His Son." He then becomes an open channel for the outflowing power of God's almighty love and will henceforth
be able to "step to and fro and find pastures," as he begins literally to feed the sheep and the lambs of God's
kingdom with the Spiritual bread of life. He will be able
to step to and fro between the two worlds and partake of
the bread and the waters of eternal life—*freely*. For such
a one the two realms are his to rejoice in and to serve in.
For such a one there is only the great, wondrous, glorified,
dynamic life! Life more abundant! Even Life Everlasting!

"Come, and partake of the Waters of Life freely," is
the eternal invitation to all men. This was revealed by
Christ for the whole race of mankind. It is not only for
the dead, but is also for the living, for "God is the God
of the living!" This is God's great gift to every child of
His!

If you have no desires for these truths and they hold
no appeal for you, if instead, you still yearn for the fulfilment of your financial dreams, or your worldly ambitions
and conquests and desires, as you long to continue in your
mortal ways, the ways of the flesh, then do not be disturbed or troubled but go your way with God's speed.

This record was not written for the sealed, orthodoxed
minds that unprogressively worship the road their ancestors

trod. Those who can only gaze in awe and reverence upon the past and its achievements are never able to fulfill their own great destiny in the eternal, ever-present NOW. These sealed ones do not realize it but they are denying God the power to operate or manifest His wondrous works in their lives. It is for this reason that the present remains unglorified and unenlightened except for those distant, dimmed, burned-out candles of the past. And man himself remains impotent and fear-filled as he stretches out his hungry, empty hands toward the ancient glories.

Each new generation was meant to build upon the generations preceding it, not lean upon them. Each was intended to accomplish all that the preceding generation accomplished and then go on to even greater works. Instead each generation has become a little more impotent as the great powers manifest in the by-gone times have slipped a little farther from his grasp, until the connecting link has become lost in obscurity.

When any individual discredits these higher truths, rejects them, denies them and fights against them because he personally has known no one who has fulfilled them, then he enters the ranks of the *"restrainers."* Such a one has sealed his own progress as he continues to be satisfied with the half-truths that were good enough for his predecessors. And as he endeavors to restrain the Light, his greatest restraint will be upon himself, for he seals the way to his own progress and his own powerful enlightenment. In the great, final analysis he will find that he has restrained the work of God not at all, "For none who make it their business to restrain the sacred draught will be able to restrain it," as the saintly writer of the Odes of Solomon proclaimed.

This draught is the waters of the sacred River of Life, the dynamic love of God and the knowledge of it and the power to send it forth until it fills the whole earth. As the Waters of that Sacred River, which was brought into the temple (of man's own being) are accepted and made use of, death and all its powers will be overcome. This mighty victory is an individual accomplishment, though it rightfully belongs to every human being on the earth. The victory is for each and every soul who will fulfill the divine measure of himself and step forth to complete his destiny.

Love must fill the hearts, the eyes, the minds and the emotions of them who become the blessed dispensers of this life-giving draught. This love must grow and expand as it gives out the healing benediction of God's almighty power of renewal—even His divine gift of Life Eternal.

I would rend the veil from your eyes that you could see but if I were to do so I would only injure you. You yourselves must grow into this higher vibration and into the knowledge of that effulgent, unspeakable glory of Christ's holy Light as your hearts open to God's divine, out-pouring love.

If you have any desire for these greater things, if mortality has left you disappointed and wanting, then begin to exercise faith by learning to *be-live* according to His promises and His laws and you will soon *know* of their truth. And *"Knowledge is power!"*

To join the ranks of the flame-shod, or the great Brotherhood of Light, one has only to bring forth that Christ Light from within, as he learns to hold himself in the outflowing glory of God's enfolding love, until he is so filled with love he becomes that love. Light will begin to fill the entire being of one who is earnest and continues in his search. As one then opens his heart and mind to love, they will be sealed against the darkness and the evils of life. Such a one becomes flame-shod as he is finally permitted to step forth purified and redeemed to fulfill his honored destiny.

The transition into the higher realm is a simple task. It requires only that one loves God with all his heart, soul, mind and strength. As one loves with the fullest extent of his own capacity, he draws the full flowing current of God's Almighty love to him. So it is that one does not need to travel, nor die, in order to have the privilege of entering into the sanctifying glory of that sacred River of Life. It flows to the individual who will perfect the gift of love in his own heart and send it out with its holy life-giving essence of renewal and quickening power.

The first and second Great Commandments, when fulfilled, contain the access to the very Tree of Life. And it is every man's right to partake of that fruit of the Tree of Life, for "that fruit is the love of God that is shed forth through the hearts of the children of men."

Love fulfills all the laws, even as Saint John so definitely proclaimed. When the laws are fulfilled, the perfection is established. Then it is that the promises must be fulfilled also. The promises and the laws are interwoven. Combined, they make up the fabric of ultimate completion. When man fulfills the laws, the fulfilled promises of glory are the only possible result.

Let your love become established, pure and unfeigned and you will have the power to step forth into the realms of the sanctified ones, gloriously beautiful, a flame-shod child of Light.

"Pray with all the energy of heart that you might be possessed of this great love." This love will grow as one desires it and practices it constantly. In practicing this love, one's bickerings, contentions, criticizing attitudes, hates and discords, are automatically dropped. They are old, ugly garments outgrown and discarded. They are old shoes cast aside for flame-shod ones, eternally beautiful, bearing the wearer into the exalted realms of a higher vibration or dimension or realm, whichever you choose to call it.

THE LIMITLESS POWER OF PRAYER

Chapter XI

Everyone who sets out upon that most noble of all quests, the quest for his own soul, or the holy grail, learns that prayer, when lifted high, beyond a thoughtless, habitual muttering or a lifeless ritual is partaking of the holy sacrament for he is having holy communion with Jesus Christ, the Lord. Prayer, when offered in love and rejoicing and praise and thanksgiving, is the time of spiritual feasting. It is the banquet of the Lord in which every man is invited to partake. One soon learns, in this true order of prayer, that the approach to God is not a whining monologue of anguished pleas, nor an accumulation of complaints, nor a thoughtless, habitual repetition of unfelt statements, strewn out like beads along a string. Prayer, when released from the heart, with feeling and spiritual awareness, becomes like incense ascending in glory to the throne of God, as explained in John's mighty book of Revelations.

Prayer is the sacred door through which the mind enters the secret chambers of the soul. It is the holy communion and is a priceless privilege for as one enters that secret closet he is always rewarded openly for having kept so sacred a tryst and partaken of the holy sacrament, the bread of life.

Prayer is also the door into the higher realm of vibration. Within prayer is contained the power to step out of the evils and dismays and disastrous tragedies of life into the joyous experiences of peace and happiness and unlimited achievement. But, the prayer must be true in its triumphant releasing as it goes forth on its vibrating glory to the very throne of God. Such prayers are endowed with the flames of exquisite, living light.

It is so much easier to approach God and have communion with Him than to gain admittance to any officious magistrate or worldly ruler or potentate. One needs no appointment, no mediator, no go-between or representative. One needs only a tender, melted, open heart and a loving reverence. When the heart is melted and opened, the hardened stone or seal is dissolved and rolled away. It is then the Light comes forth, the great Christ Light, resurrected and released from its tomb within man.

It is the broken or open heart that is the only offering worthy of so dynamic an event. For as Christ so definitely revealed, "The only acceptable sacrifice that would be received from then on and henceforth would be the sacrifice of a yielding, broken or open heart." Prayer, in its true form, is but the opening of the heart for it is through the heart that one partakes of the spiritual feast of the divine and holy sacrament.

If man will only open his mind to comprehend the power and the glorious privilege of prayer, he will open the doors into the higher realms of divine power.

Prayer is a breathtaking experience for him who comprehends its true order and releases its unlimited power. Prayer cannot fail. It may be possible that at first one's prayers may not change outside conditions to suit the mortal request of the individual. This however does not mean that prayer has failed or remained unheard. If the prayer is continued one automatically begins to "exercise the great and mighty faith" that brings forth the seemingly impossible results. If the prayer one offers is held in the consciousness and is sent forth whenever one has a free moment to direct his mind toward it, something must give. It may be that the prayer will change the individual to suit the condition instead of the condition being changed to suit the individual. If this be the method used in answering one's prayer, then it will be the individual who will be exalted into a higher condition and the outside circumstances will then come under subjection to him as he rises above it. This is power.

Most completely physical mortals would rather perish than change themselves or their habits or their way of thinking. Prayer, if understood, can change one's attitude to meet any condition and so give him the power to rise triumphantly above it as he learns to ride upon the storm. Prayer can blend one's will so completely with the Will of God that only perfection can result. But in this transition one must learn the true meaning and order of prayer. Prayer is the door into the higher realms. Prayer is the holy communion with God as one partakes of His Spiritual banquet.

As one enters the secret chamber of his own soul, to praise and adore and worship, he opens the door to the universe and will receive blessings so great they will surpass any small, worldly desires he could possibly have wished for. He will be rewarded openly for such holy communion. He will receive blessings of health of body and mind and soul. He will be given the happiness and the peace that passeth understanding. As one prays just for the joy of praying, in adoring worship, he will develop the love that fulfills all laws. In fulfilling the law of love he will bring forth the great Christ Light until he is filled with Light and comprehends all things. He will then be admitted into the Church of the Firstborn and join with the great Brotherhood of Light. This is accomplished by love fulfilling the laws of one's own being as he brings forth the Light of Christ. Then he is born of the Spirit. In fulfilling the perfect law of love he is thereby immersed in that River of Life or the waters of love and is born of the waters.

It is as necessary to one's well-being to meet together with God often, in this secret closet of his own soul, and partake of Christ's holy sacrament and feast on His spiritual food, as it is necessary to partake of physical food in order to keep the body functioning. The soul requires this banquet of food *often,* as often as one partakes of his physical meals. Prayer is the time of partaking of the great feast of the Lord. Therefore a time should be set apart for this spiritual meal, as definitely established as the appointed time of one's daily meals. It is in this continued awareness that one steps out, flame-shod, upon the path of unspeakable power.

Prayer is truly a divine privilege. It is indeed a time of holy communion as one learns to "be still" as well as to express his own desires. Prayer contains the power to prepare one for his own divine fulfilment. Prayer is the gift of communion as one learns to commune with God in the feast of the Spirit. It is a time of releasing those inner songs of joyous gratitude and loving adoration that vibrate across the universe, blending with the great universal symphony of creation.

True prayer carries with it thanks and praise and love. True prayer is not a wailing complaint of saddened anguish. And again, quoting from Malachi: "This ye have done again, covering the altar of the Lord with tears, with weeping, and with crying out, insomuch that he regardeth not the offering any more, or receiveth it with good will at your hands." Prayer was not meant to be a burdened affliction or a dirge of anguished pleading. True prayer is a song of triumphant glory as one sends out his own vibrations of praise to mingle with the creative song of God—the New Song that fulfills a law of its own as the individual is re-created into God's perfect plan of eternal glory. As one prays thus, he will find that all blessings flow back to him along those opened channels of praise, love and gratitude. Praise and love and gratitude are the opened channels through which his blessings return unto him multiplied and complete.

True prayer must always contain the divine attitude of thanks for past blessings and for all present ones. The "Beatitudes," as Christine Mercie revealed in her little booklet, "Sons of God," means that one must *be* that *attitude*. And gratitude is the great-attitude for it is the greatest of all.

Always approach God in this greatest attitude and your blessings will be multiplied and enlarged. Gratitude is the law of multiplication in the physical as well as the spiritual realm. It is the law of increase. Self-pity dispels all blessings for it smothers the very vibrations that would lift the request or prayer to God. There is nothing creative in self-pity or in any of the negative attributes of darkness. In order to multiply and to use the laws of creation, one must begin to express the creative laws of the universe—which are——love and praise and gratitude. These three contain the great "Lost Chord" of creation. Within these three powers is contained the power of creation as one joins the strength of his soul in the release of that New Song, that only the righteous can learn, the great, creative song of the Universe.

Self-pity and sadness and doubting and any of the negative traits or habits of mortality, instantly block off the vibrations that fulfill one's requests as well as block off the power of one's own reception. Gratitude enlarges all gifts and all possessions and all blessings. When gratitude is established within one, that one opens his whole heart, soul and mind to the exquisite glory of abundance and increasing joy, until he receives a very fulness of joy. "And joy is of the saints and none can put it on save they alone!" Or, according to the more recent scriptures: "He who is thankful in all things shall be made glorious! And the things of this earth shall be added unto him an hundredfold; yea, more!"

As one continues in the search for his own soul, he reaches that point where he *knows* and contacts that divine Spark of God implanted within. And by the time he reaches It, It will have matured until it fills his own being and he will "be filled with the fulness of God," as Paul promised in Ephesians. This holy seed grows according to man's awareness of it and according to the spiritual food it receives, which is obtained through the holy communion. As this holy spark or seed is developed from within, and brought forth, it naturally must, in time, fill one's entire being, even as the germ of the chick must grow until it fills the shell. Then it is that one becomes filled with Light and comprehends all things and becomes "one with God," as Christ so earnestly enjoined. This is the point of power. This unfolding and development of the divine and holy Seed of God, until it fills the entire being of man, is the coming forth of the "Father within to begin to do the works," as Christ testified.

As one reaches this point of development it becomes easy for him to "let go and let God." Such a one learns to speak no word save God commands it. And in thus learning to control his own run-away tongue he will have brought his run-away thoughts into a refined point of obedience. Through harboring only love-filled thoughts he becomes a perfect man and is henceforth able to bridle and control the whole body, as St. James promised. He will be able to control every living atom and cell and organ and gland of it. He will have the power to step beyond decay and death into the life more abundant—even Life Eternal!

Prayer works through natural law. Prayer IS the natural law of man's being. Prayer is the holy communion man holds with his Maker, if his prayers are not defiled by doubts and fears and negative thoughts and complaints. As long as one holds naught but sadness and mourning forth, his thoughts are not upon God, nor are his "eyes single to the glory of God." Instead his attention is held upon the earth level and upon his own mortal condition. Such prayers are earthbound and hold in them only the darkness of mortality. Such thoughts are limited and such prayers are weakened by the individual's own dismal attitudes. But even then such prayers must be answered.

But there are prayer levels of fulfilment and each prayer ascends to its own level—and is answered from that level.

Prayers of love and gratitude and rejoicing are prayers of unlimited power for they are already allied with the dynamic power of faith and are therefore completely limitless in their scope as they ascend instantly to the Highest.

When sent out from the heart, prayers are the true expression of a man's own soul. True prayer is the manifestation of the soul's sublime assertion when released with real intent. Prayer is the action of the soul as it reaches out to partake of the spiritual food of the Almighty in the holy communion of God, the divine sacrament.

And prayer, no matter what its level, is man's acknowledgement of his belief in God, no matter how weak that belief may be. The prayers that are not contaminated by sadness and whimpering self-pity, are embued with faith and allied with limitless power. When these prayers are clothed in love and glorified by praise and gratitude, they have immediate access to God's divine attention. The "New Song, which none but the righteous can learn," is a song of singing joyous triumph. It is the song of Creation. This divine song holds within it the powers of the Universe as it is released through man's own open heart. Such prayers are the expression and the release of that superb, dynamic, glorified song of Creation. And, in that creative song of gratitude and rejoicing and love, are the full powers to create and bring forth the desired requests to the individual.

In fears and negation and sadness, "the New Song" is not released, hence, the powers of creation are unexpressed. The negative attitudes and vibrations of individuals without hope, do not contain even one note, let alone the melody of that great creative song of fulfilment within their somber tones. In the negative attitudes, the sadness and sighing complaints, only the vibrations of destruction are held, not the forces and powers of creation.

Within man's own attitude is held the caliber of his prayer and the level from which it will be answered. Learn the New Song, the song of inner praise and love and gratitude and you will be not only in tune with the great creative song of the Universe, you will be a participant in its release. Such prayers contain only beauty and power in their release and the powers of creation are set into motion to bring forth the complete fulfilment.

One cannot become the Master of this greatest of all symphonies in a moment or a day. But, man himself is the instrument on which the dynamic Song of Creation must be played in its divine release. The instrument, the divine innermost being of man, when first put into use, may need tuning and adjusting. And the individual who releases that divine melody will need some training to make sure that no negative, sour notes are released to mar the melody of divine Creation.

If the condition is not changed through prayer and supplication, then the man will be changed to surmount the condition—to rise above it and to overcome it—or come up over it. It is then one learns to ride upon the storm instead of being submerged by it. Such a one has gained the complete mastery. He therefore becomes the Master of every condition. The very changing of the man, instead of the condition, is often the greatest miracle of all. It is then, man himself, can outgrow or surmount the condition through the power of prayer, as God answers that prayer openly.

Some never recognize this answer to their prayers. Some even reject this greater blessing as they refuse to let go of their own pre-conceived ideas as to how their request should be answered. As one learns to "let go and let God," the perfect answer will be worked out. It is, then, for man to grow into that answer, which is always the only perfect answer.

As prayer becomes a part of one's life, that is, true prayer, not just habitual mutterings with much repetition, but a sacrament of holy communion, one becomes attuned to the higher vibrations of love and is prepared to receive divine guidance and personal instruction for his everyday life. His petty, selfish, often warped little desires become purified and exalted as they expand into divine desires.

Prayers that are sent forth with the strength of the mind and the integrity of the soul and the love of the heart behind them, are released by power and must be answered. They become engraved upon the sub-conscious mind and are established as a reality. Then, through adding the ingredient of love and praise and thanks, they are exalted into a higher vibratory realm or condition and are established upon the super-conscious mind, where all power and fulfilment is contained. They are spiritually intensified through love and praise to the point of complete fulfilment, for in the love and praise and gratitude the Creative forces of the Universe are set instantly into motion. This higher law of prayer and the manner of its fulfilment and the method of its release, must be comprehended, for the need for such prayers is at hand. Such prayers must be answered, for this is the law of God.

"Whatsoever you ask for when you pray, believe that you receive it and you shall have it!" Christ never asked for anything without thanking God for the answer to His request even as He asked. As in the case of Lazarus' raising, He thanked God for hearing Him and acknowledged that He was aware that God always heard Him. Anyone who prays from the depth of his soul, instead of from his disorganized mind or from his lips, will *know* that God hears his prayer. He also knows that God will answer that prayer in His own way and His own wisdom. As one accepts this answer, he will learn to blend his will into the Will of God, as he rejoices and gives thanks that God has heard and is answering his request.

As one gives forth thanks and praise and love, the light is increased until it is brought forth in its fulness. And in the Light all doubts are conquered, all darkness is banished and the veil is rent. It is then, one is permitted to enter the realm of infinite power and fulfilment.

The road of prayer is the most satisfying, rewarding Way of all ways. It is the great Inner Way—the way of Inner Communion—the Way of the great Christ Light. It is the Way Christ marked, as he asked that man worship God with all his mind, heart and soul. It is the dynamic path He trod, the road of fulfilment as one develops eyes single to the glory of God, for in God's glory is man's own glory held. And such shall truly be made glorious.

True prayer lifts or exalts one into the higher realm of spiritual vision and power and joy. This is the state wherein one fulfills all the laws and keeps all the commandments, for love will become perfected in him. Then it is that one's love becomes so great he desires only God's will to be accomplished. It is in this final relinquishing of one's own will to the great ecstatic song of love that he realizes all the little petty things he once desired are empty and meaningless and outgrown, even as the toys of his childhood. One relinquishes these mortal, physical, childish requests with a great joy, even as he would discard his old, worn-out garments for new ones. The small desires are completely outgrown and left behind as they are replaced by breath-taking, dynamic ones that hold the keys of all power and all joy and all happiness.

Yes. Prayer changes the man, as it exalts both the individual and the condition, until all things become perfect in his life and his surroundings. As man is changed, by true prayer, he is lifted above the condition and the condition itself will melt into a conformity of pattern that no longer has the power to rule, but is ruled over by the mastering triumph of exalted progress.

In the "letting go and letting God," one permits God to begin to do His great and mighty works. And it is true that "God's Will has never been contrary to man's will. It has been man's will that has been contrary to God's Will." As man has stubbornly held out against the fulfilling of his own perfection and infinite happiness, he remained impotent, miserable and completely without power. His strength may be placed in a gun, in a speeding car, or in some mechanical creation, instead of being centered in the divine powers of Creation. Man's own mechanical devices and instruments and machines have out-brained him and put him to an open shame. For those great unspeakable powers that will subdue himself, his earthly conditions and the world itself, man must begin to contact the divine forces dormant in his own soul, as he begins to work with God.

"God's holy Will holds within it the glorified, exalted destiny of each child of earth. "For this is my work and my glory, to bring to pass the immortality and eternal life of man." Within this eternal life is contained all the happiness, the joy and the power of exalting glory heaven holds.

The Kingdom of Heaven is a condition. It is a condition of exalting all the conditions, as the individual is exalted into a higher vibration and all circumstances surrounding him. It is brought about or brought forth by one's releas-

ing the inner joy and love in a song of everlasting gratitude that completely fills his being—and increases until it
fills his life. This is how God's will is fulfilled on earth
even as it is in heaven. As the flesh is exalted and lifted
to the vibrational level of the spirit within, the physical,
outside plane takes on the glory of the inside heaven. And
so is fulfilled that perfect prayer, "Thy Will be done on
earth even as it is in heaven." And "The *kingdom of heaven
is within you!*" The way into it is through prayer.

"Seek first the Kingdom of God and its righteousness
and all things will be added unto you." Seek first His
Kingdom and learn the right-use or application of its divine laws and all things will be added unto you—and all
powers.

You may desire to know when these things will be accomplished.

For many they have already been fulfilled.

For you they will be completed when you are ready. In
the spiritual realm there is only the great eternal NOW!
In the eternal, "time is not!" The eternal is the ever living,
vibrating NOW!

Youth looks into the future—waiting for fulfilment. Age
looks into the past, thinking it was there, and fearing they
have missed it. Both youth and age and those between
have missed it, for it is not in time, but in attitude. The
fulfilment is centered in one's *be living,* as they follow the
Way Christ marked and live according to the pattern He
gave.

"And Jesus answering, saith unto them, Have faith in
God. For verily I say unto you, that whosoever shall say
unto this mountain, Be thou removed and be thou cast
into the sea; and *shall not doubt in his heart,* but shall

be-live (be and live accordingly) that those things which he saith shall come to pass, he shall have whatsoever he saith. Therefore I say unto you, what things soever ye desire, when ye pray, believe that you receive them, and ye shall have them." (Mark 11:22-24)

As the true method of prayer is established within one and he develops the power to believe without doubting, everything he can possibly ask for will be fulfilled, for then his requests will be purified and exalted according to his faith and his own exalted attitude of mind. And perhaps, instead of asking for some trivial, little, mediocre request, he will ask what before seemed impossible. He may desire to remove some mountain looming in his own pathway as he seeks to climb that upward trail of completion. He may desire to remove some almost insurmountable weakness from his own being as it hampers his progress—and by his prayer of faith that mountain can and will be removed.

As one learns the power of prayer and the method of its glorious release, his requests will transcend into the desires that would seem to be utterly fantastic and completely impossible, perhaps even blasphemous, to him in his present, mortal state of uninspired, unspiritual plodding. As one advances, he will think greater thoughts, have greater desires, reach for higher goals and will realize that the great fulfilment of himself will have to fulfill the promises Christ left behind, the promise to be able to do all the works which Christ did——and then go on to even the greater works.

As one progresses he must grow into the knowledge and the belief in such powers. And he learns that prayer is the door to the greater things as he learns "to pray without ceasing."

Prayer and all the limitless powers it contains, are man's, as he learns to use them. As one learns to add to his prayers the song of ecstasy in an anthem of eternal praise and love and gratitude, he will be singing that glorious New Song at the very throne of God. And in the melody of that exalted Symphony of Creation all the forces and powers of creation are released to fulfill his divine requests. Love and Praise and thanksgiving open up the channels along which one's blessings return in all their fulfilling power of completion.

This is the great Inner Path of your own fulfilling! This higher Way is the Way that cannot fail. This higher Way contains "the New Song" which none but the righteous can learn. It is not a song of words but of vibrations. The vibrations of love and joyous praise and the vibrations of thanksgiving exalted into a chorus of dynamic gratitude, contain the vibrant tones of Creation. These tones combined are the "Lost Chord!" These great vibrational overtones of love and praise and thanks contain the released melody of the Celestial Song of Creation, the divine symphony of eternal triumph.

This New Song, the divine Song of creation is the Song of exultant victory as evolving mortals triumph over drab mortality in their upward march toward godhood.

THE TREASURES IN HEAVEN

Chapter XII

Man's suffering is not caused as a punishment by God, as mankind has been taught to believe. Shocks and hurts and suffering are caused when man's will is set rigidly against the Will of God. God's will enfolds all creation in love and tenderness as all things are moved forward by its fulfilling, unless one's personal will is set in resistance and selfish determination to accomplish its own greedy or adverse little desires.

In God's divine Will is held the perfection of all things and all conditions. Mortal vision has not been lifted high enough to become "single to the glory of God." Mortal men exert their own immature wills according to their degree of comprehension—or lack of it. If one sets his heart and mind upon what he personally wills or desires, he is not considering God's will at all, nor is he viewing that divine, higher glory, to which his eyes are supposed to become single.

Those who can lift their vision above their own little, mortal, selfish, personal desires and lusts will begin to develop the higher vision. Within that exalted view one's eyes become "single to God's glory." And as one begins to behold the glory of God he begins to reflect and to take on that glory. "Who can interpret the wonders of the

Lord? For he who could interpret would be dissolved and would become that which is interpreted."

When one uses his will to blend with the exalted, perfect Will of God the little mortal self steps into its maturity and all things work together for his good. This is love in action. Such a one achieves the power to step beyond his own little physical lusts and desires to conform his hopes and desires into the great Will or Plan of the Almighty—which plan is the unfolding of himself in divine perfection.

As one lifts his vision to behold the glory of God he "Becomes filled with light and there is no darkness in him. And that soul who is filled with light comprehends all things. And God will unveil His face unto him. It will be in His own time and in His own way and according to His own will." In God's Will is the great perfection held. When His Will is permitted to complete its work then will the results be fully accomplished. The time is established as the time when man lets God's Will fulfill its perfect works.

It is in man's own determined resistance, his self-willed actions and violent, discordant reactions, that all man's sufferings and misfortunes lie. Man's hurts and anguish and almost impossible conditions of desolation are the results of his contrary efforts as he sets his own bleak, distorted, over-indulged, puny little will in opposition to God's holy plan for his own perfection as well as for the perfection and glorification of the world.

When an individual can train his "eyes to become single to the glory of God" his vision will become exalted or lifted to the higher reality. As one learns to blend his will into the Will of God, all things begin to work together for his good. This is God's great law of completion as all things begin to be fulfilled in the individual—and for him. As one relinquishes his will in a vibrant, living surrender he proves his love. Until this is accomplished love has been perhaps, only a desire, a belief in one's own self-righteousness, a fanatical acclamation of words, a yearning hope and yet remained an unfulfilled achievement. When love is perfected the little personal will is exalted into a triumphant, glorious, exalted vibration that blends with the Will of God in everlasting power and divine accomplishment.

To surrender one's will does not make one spineless nor does it turn him into an inanimate, listless stodgy, a "rubber stamp" or a weak little "yes man." As one's will is purified and one's love exalted to the degree of such infinite, glorious understanding he becomes vibrant and alive and filled with the ineffable powers of eternity.

In the Will of God there is nothing withheld—no powers, no glory, no happiness and no unanswered longings.

I first beheld the wonder and the perfection of the things Christ holds within His holy hands when lovely Linda lay at death's door—and was healed instantly as I relinquished my will to Him. I beheld the glory of the gifts He holds out to a world so lost in darkness and lack and misery. I saw the unspeakable magnitude of His plans as He waits in tender patience to place His limitless powers into the hands of those who will only lift their vision high enough to comprehend and to desire gifts of such unutterable magnitude.

There is no need for lack or for illness or for want and poverty and anguish. These things have never been a part of God's plan, nor are they contained within His Holy Will. He is waiting anxiously to bestow His powers upon any who will desire them and *be-lieve* the laws required in order to produce the necessary faith and develop the required love. There is the power to supply every need, to heal every illness, to bring to pass every noble desire, accomplish every task and complete every glorious hope. All the ineffable powers of fulfilling and completion are awaiting man's acceptance of them. There is not only the power to live nobly and happily, as one learns to rule his life in perfect beauty and divine satisfaction, but there is power to reach out into eternity and exert an influence upon the very stars.

Such were the things that were revealed to me so long ago. And since I have beheld the actuality of their truth. At that time I could not understand, for then, I believed that each man had been created to fulfill his full measure of suffering and pain and misery without even a glimmer of happiness or joy.

And I beheld that man esteemed His priceless gifts and powers as of no value, casting them aside for cheap, red glass beads—or for the worthless trash the world holds forth.

And so man suffers and is distraught and is at war with himself as he battles against all that is perfect and divine.

"As one learns obedience by the things which he suffers, the suffering ends." This suffering has been caused, not by God's punishing hands, but by man's own created, adverse vibrations as he has set them in contrary motion against his own fulfilment.

Each individual desires to reform and remake everyone else but himself. He desires others to fulfill the perfection he holds within his own inner being, but not for "all the king's horses and all the king's men," or for the king's whole realm, for that matter, will he make the least effort to change himself. Each man is in a deep rut of self-satisfaction and semi-petrified unprogressiveness, or blind indifference.

Man has erroneously believed his joy and happiness is contained in outside circumstances and possessions and conditions. Man does not yet realize that there is no permanent joy or lasting value contained in the acquisition of worldly goods. "Even if a man gains the whole world, and loses his own soul, of what profit would it be?" The loss of a man's soul may be contained in his failure to contact that sacred soul, housed within himself.

That desolate, yearning cry of the soul is not fulfilled by the accumulation of worldly wealth, or academic or worldly knowledge. "The learning of the world is foolishness to the Lord." If knowledge, that has been gleaned from other men's thoughts, as one has buried himself in books and schools and libraries, is foolishness, then that one has only made himself a receptacle of accumulated foolishness. What a lamentable waste.

And all the treasures one may gather, and all the wealth one may hoard, and all the lands one may claim can never really be possessed by any man at all. "The earth is the Lord's and the fulness thereof." One can only hold the substances of this earth in stewardship, not in ownership, as he will be held accountable for the use he puts that stewardship to. He has only the right to use the treasures of this earth temporarily. They are only borrowed and for a very short time—at the longest—the length of his own life. The treasures of the earth can never actually belong to any mortal man. Each generation has staked its claims and in turn has had to relinquish them.

And all material treasures are subject to moth and rust and to loss by thieves. Even if one has accumulated belongings which he may so securely hold in his greedy clutch none can part him from a single coin, death will come and pry his fingers loose and his hands will be emptied of even the smallest grain of sand.

All that truly belongs to any man is his own individual experiences as he has acted out his daily life, or as he selects and lives the part he plays, and chooses the way he plays it. In the unfolding of the character he creates will be contained his own values in his actions toward others and his re-actions to their needs.

One may think his treasures are gathered by the many church meetings he attends, the contributions he makes or the donations he contributes. In this thought he errs. Even while a man is performing such acts he may be so filled with hate or selfish scheming he has not lifted a single thought or vibration in one degree of increased love. Worse, he may be resentful and covetous of that which he gives, to be seen of men. Such outward rituals and contributions and services have no value for the individual. They may even be considered as evil. And certainly they are in vain. "If a man gives all that he has to the poor and even his body to be burned, and has not love, it is as nothing."

What actually belongs to the individual are only the things he has built into himself. The virtues one has developed become an everlasting part of the man. Not even his physical body goes with him, unless he has exalted it to the spiritual height of his own divine potentialities. No man can lay a permanent claim to a single nickle or a handful of dust, or even to a chest or a chamber full of jewels. All that is his, by right of permanent possession, are the ideals he holds, the kindness he feels, the good he has done, the love he has developed and the tolerance, patience, understanding, compassion, integrity and courage he has established within himself. These treasures alone are his own. These are the treasures in heaven, the priceless, everlasting wealth that is eternally his as he has embedded their virtues into the fibres of his own innermost being. These are the treasures of heaven—"The heaven that is within." After these riches are established within a man they can never be forfeited, or relinquished or destroyed. Neither moth nor rust can claim them, nor can thieves break through and steal.

But until these treasures are permanently established, as a definite part of the individual, he himself can relinquish or forfeit them by changing his attitudes and his thought habits as he yields to temptations and animal lusts. If, however, he holds to a noble course long enough these virtues become his own—and *he becomes them.*

One does not need to die in order to reap the reward of his good. These priceless treasures of integrity are his constant source of strength and well-being. He can draw upon them in every emergency as they give him the power to meet and triumph over every misfortune, vicissitude or disaster.

Money in the bank? Yes. They are that and much, much more. They are the treasures within oneself that fulfill and answer his every urgent need. They increase with use instead of diminishing. They grow brighter and more valuable with usury and the principle and the profits belong to the owner of these divine treasures of heaven—"The kingdom within."

Anything that is outside of an individual is not his own,

though he may lay claim to it in his foolish arrogance. Only the things that have become an actual part of one's self are his own. It is the noble aspirations, the kindly deeds, the unselfish actions, the exalted thoughts that are one's permanent possessions and his only real treasures. One takes on the vibrations of his own burning desires, his intense thought vibrations. He becomes these things as they are stashed away into the living vaults of his own being. These dynamic things he stores into his kingdom of heaven, even the everlasting tones of all that he has done and all that he has thought and felt are his own. These vibrations are the eternal reality of his true possessions.

And so, it may be possible that one is only the owner of all the evils and wickedness he has brought forth in his selfishness and lusts or his slothfulness or hates. Such a one has no bank account to draw upon. He has no treasures to insure him any comfort or happiness either in this world— or in the world to come. He has only an accumulation of debts encumbered by his unjust actions, his lusts and jealousies and hates, or by his own inert slothfulness. Such a one has mortgaged his soul—and his debts increase with compounded interest.

The treasures of heaven continually pay their dividends and the one who possesses them constantly reaps their rewards. His every day is enhanced and worthwhile as he draws upon the interest from his treasures to fortify and ennoble his labors even while assuring him of success and honor in all his mortal dealings.

It is not the visible treasures of earth that have any value. And it is certainly not the treasures of this world to which a man can lay permanent claim. A man is only wealthy who has "laid up for himself treasures in heaven, where neither moth nor rust doth corrupt, and where thieves cannot break through and steal." And where death has no power to pry his fingers loose as he is left clutching nothing but his dismal regrets and an overdue mortgage.

The virtues one develops within himself, the caliber of his mercy, the honesty of his dealings with his fellowmen, the worth of his word, the integrity of his actions, the nobility of his thoughts, these are his treasures as they are laid up in the kingdom of his own heaven, the kingdom within himself. These alone are his. His wealth consists entirely of his virtues.

"Because thou sayest, I am rich and increased with goods, and have need of nothing; and knowest not that thou art wretched, and miserable, and poor, and blind, and naked (because none of these things are your own, regardless of your claims);

"I counsel thee to buy of me gold tried in the fire (of your own soul), that thou mayest be rich; and white raiment, that thou mayest be clothed, and that the shame of thy nakedness do not appear; and anoint thy eyes with eyesalve, that thou mayest see." (Rev. 3:17-18).

The gold that is tried in the fire (of a man's own soul)? Yes. That gold is the only wealth any individual can possibly possess permanently. He who possesses such wealth is rich indeed. This wealth, one is invited to purchase from God, is paid for by the golden coins of love as his devotion expands. This wealth is purchased by unselfish actions, by kindness to a neighbor, an acquaintance, a friend— or better still, *an enemy*, multiplied and continued and enlarged until every act is noble and beautiful—and divine. This wealth is purchased by the golden coins of tenderness, by the inspired moments of true prayer, by one's degree of gratitude and in his exulting praise and inner awareness.

These treasures of the soul exalt a man into a noble person of goodness and honor and power. They also release into his hands the keys of abundance as his joys multiply and his happiness increases.

Whatever a man builds into his own character becomes his permanent possession, his indestructible riches, his everlasting treasures of boundless wealth. These treasures are beyond decay and destruction and the reach of thieves.

All worldly treasures, that are accumulated in greed and selfishness and mis-directed energies, are outside of the individual and therefore are not his own. They are treasures he can lay no actual claim to, "For the earth is the Lord's and the fulness thereof." The worldly wealth one may lay claim to cannot possibly become his own. All that is his are the attributes and the selfish desires that were used in acquiring such outside possessions. These treasures of the earth are only a counterfeit, worthless collection of value-less, temporary duration. And for these worthless, impermanent possessions one may have forfeited his own soul.

The only real, lasting treasures are the ones which a man has gathered into himself as he has enriched that divine "Kingdom of heaven—which is within."

Man has ignored the invitation to lay up for himself treasures in heaven because he believes they are too remote. He thinks they only pertain to and have value in another day—another life—another dimension. Man does not realize that the treasures he builds into his own character are his to enjoy and to rejoice in every moment of his present life as he walks with his head held high, unbowed by shame and unencumbered by inferior qualifications.

And the treasures that are of the most value are the

kind actions one performs when no record is made of them. They are the actions one does when he believes no one is looking. These are the works that one does in secret, not letting his right hand know what his left hand is doing. This sacred silence means that he can share his deeds with no one, not even the mate of his bosom. If he so much as shares these actions with a living soul he has, in a measure or even fully, reaped his reward from the admiring approval of his fellow man. If he retains his silence he deposits the greatest treasures of all into that divine kingdom of heaven. Such deposits bring the eternal rewards that reach beyond all earthly values.

This silence is also true of those who perform little unworthy, sneaky acts when they think no one is watching. These sneaky little actions are the most detrimental of all to a man's soul. To counteract these weak, immoral inclinations of man the confessionals were established in medieval times. These confessionals hold, at best, only the weak power of a smeared erasure in their effort to supplant virtues for vice. They contain no beneficent value whatsoever unless they establish living virtues within the heart of the penetant.

Within each man is the kingdom, or the bank, into which his merits are deposited. In the next world a man is not judged by his possessions or his learning or by his earthly honors or positions. A man is judged by what he IS. What he *is* is the only measure of valuation. He STANDS FORTH the sum total of all that he has thought and felt and done. He is nothing more and nothing less. And his virtues are his own—and *he is them.*

"The white raiment," which man is counseled to buy of God, that the shame of his nakedness or worthlessness

may not appear," is the great Christ Light as it is brought
forth from within. Those who develop and release this
"Light of Christ, which has been given to abide in every
man who cometh into the world," will be clothed in its
glory. And they will belong henceforth to the great Brotherhood of Light, the holy anointed ones who are Christ's
true followers.

That apparel of effulgent power and beauty is brought
forth from within as one "begins to lay up for himself his
treasures in heaven." That glorified white raiment is the
outflowing interest that accrues from one's deposits, made
in love and gratitude and praise.

These treasures of heaven are the divine gifts and qualities a man develops as he releases the hidden, God-given
potentialities within himself and actually becomes them.
These are the treasures indeed—the everlasting, glorious
gifts of God. These are the gifts and powers that God
holds forth to all. They are all in His plan as He waits
patiently for man to accept them.

In God's holy Will the unfolding plan of glory and
perfection and eternal joy and everlasting happiness and
unimaginable power works out for the individual's complete fulfilment. This will be accomplished whenever the
individual opens his mind and heart to comprehend and
begins to co-operate. Or when he "anoints his eyes with
eyesalve that he might begin to see"—"with eyes single
to the glory of God!"

The perfect plan for every man's unfolding is contained
within the man himself. He lays up these unspeakable
powers and gifts as his mind opens to behold them and as
he develops them and thus permanently establishes them
within himself in complete awareness.

"For it is given to abide in you, the record of heaven, the peaceable things of immortal glory; the Comforter; the truth of all things; that which quickeneth all things, and maketh alive all things; that which knoweth all things and hath all power."

These unspeakable powers are contained within the individual and are brought forth with the Light of Christ and with the comprehension and development of that sacred, divine Seed of God as man brings forth this most holy of all gifts. Within the divine Will of God is contained the perfection of every child of earth. When a man can so lift his will that it blends with God's holy Will his love will be perfected. When, in complete relinquishment, one can truthfully say, "Not my will, but thine be done!" His love will be proved and his own fulfilment be accomplished.

In, and through, the gift of love the power of faith is fulfilled and becomes *knowledge.* In and through love all things are transmuted into their highest excellence. By love man himself is transformed and translated from a grubby, earth-bound mortal into a true son, clothed in everlasting light.

Prove your love by blending your will into the holy Will of God and by such devotion you can easily purchase the gold tried in the fire and the white raiment and all the gifts and powers ever promised or given unto the children of men. And they will become your own.

Within that holy spark or Seed of God that lies dormant within man is held His complete Will and the full perfection of His divine plan for the individual's complete fulfilment and everlasting glory. Every virtue established within is only the awakening of those inner traits of splendor as one brings forth that divine, immaculate Conception contained right within himself—his own inborn divinity.

As one begins to store up for himself treasures in heaven he will soon realize the power and speed with which they multiply and accumulate is astonishingly, almost overwhelmingly gratifying. He will soon be able to sit back and watch himself grow into his own truest excellence. He will discover that he is indeed the treasure house of all that is beautiful and worthy and desirable. He will know that the pure gold, which is the only gold to which he can ever rightly lay claim, is the gold that has been tried in the purging fires within his own soul. And the white raiment, which is purchased with the golden coins of his own devotion, is the glorified Christ Light as it is brought forth to completely enfold him.

Rejoice in these great, dynamic treasures of fulfilment as heaven yields its wealth and its unlimited interest—an hundred-fold! Yea! More!

As one stores up the lasting treasures, that cannot be destroyed or stolen or forfeited by death, he will know of the priceless value of these divine gifts and will walk in the majesty and the security and the power of their strength. Such a one will know the value of the true wealth and receive the everlasting riches and be "arrayed as even Solomon, in all his glory, never dreamed of being." He will be arrayed in Light, or the white raiment of everlasting achievement and worth and power.

Such a one will be himself, without shame or pretense as he STANDS FORTH, endowed with the treasures of divinity and perfection enfolding him—a glorified son of God!

"Labor not for the things that perish," or for worldly wealth. He who labors for the things of this world is not laboring for God. Neither is he laboring for himself, as he has mistakenly believed. He is spending his time and his strength and his energies to labor for mammon, or for the world. And mammon will reap the fruits of his labors as he is finally required to relinquish the last worthless farthings of his life's efforts and returns them back to their original source—the earth.

A man is required to live honorably, to live up to his obligations to society, to keep himself and his loved ones fed and cared for and supplied with the necessities of life. This is required of him. And this he may do. No one has the right to expect others to feed and clothe him and supply his needs. For-shame to those who believe they have the right to live on the physical labors of their fellowmen as they store up their hoards of wealth. It is when one's worldly acquisitions begin to take over his life and his mind and his affections that an individual reaches the danger point where his soul relinquishes its right of supremacy and becomes the slave of his greeds and evils as he serves mammon. He is no longer free. No longer has he time or understanding to labor for the everlasting treasures, which alone can become his own.

As one uses his spare time, not to think up new ways to make more money, but to serve and worship God, he is laying up for himself the treasures within the kingdom of himself. Then it is that mammon finally loses its claim. That man who worships God with all his heart, all his mind and with all his soul will be released from the earthly demands and requirements, "So that all things will begin to be added unto him, and he will no longer need to labor for the things that perish," for food and clothing and shelter and the physical needs of the flesh. Such a progressing one will be released from the earthly demands and requirements for he will have overcome the earth and all things pertaining to it.

Every true and lasting treasure of worth belongs to him who lays up the eternal virtues of patience, goodness, kindness, compassion, virtue, tolerance, mercy, generosity, understanding and dynamic, everlasting love within his own heart. These divine treasures are much more than words. They are the true realities. They are the immortal treasures of timeless value. They are infinite and endless. They are more than thoughts and habits and desires. These are released, living vibrations which continually flow out from the very inner essence of a man's own being as they become indestructibly established within. *These are the MAN in his fulness and completion* as he steps forth clothed in the light and radiance of his own divine fulfilment. These are his treasures.

As one, thus arrayed in the divine vibrations of glory, steps across into the higher realms, he by-passes all inferior groups and levels and is ushered instantly into the highest—or the exalted dominion of his own merits. He takes his treasures with him. They are himself. And none can claim such treasures except he who has earned them.

Treasures in heaven? Yes. Virtues of beauty and power and everlasting glory—these alone are his own. And he is them. These are not the sham, counterfeit virtues of the hypocrite who spends his life and time in deceiving himself and others with his sanctimonious self-righteousness. This is the true righteousness which is established by emotions and thoughts and actions and eternal love as one worships and adores, with eyes single to the glory of God.

Man, "lay up for yourself treasures in heaven, where neither moth nor rust doth corrupt and where theives cannot break through and steal, for where your treasure is there will your heart be also." If your treasures are within the kingdom of yourself you will be rich indeed and no individual or power will ever be able to rob you of your wealth. It will be your own and you will become the divine being of your true self as your own pattern of divinity is completed and fulfilled.

The gold one is invited to purchase of God, that he may be rich, is the spiritual gold that has been tried in the fires of his own divine soul. This gold, when purified and stilled, becomes the pool of glory, the mirror that reflects out into the universal substance the vision or desire a man images into it. This is the gift of imagination perfected into its highest excellence and full purpose of functioning. This pool of pure, spiritual gold, at the center of the soul, as explained in *Temple of God*, must become stilled with the inner stillness. "Be *still* and know that I Am God!"

This is the stillness that is expressed in the divine, holy gift of *peace*—"The peace that passeth understanding." This is the peace God offered to the world with the gift of His Son. This is the peace Christ reaffirmed as He offered it in His last, gentle words, "My peace I give unto you, not as the world giveth, give I unto you." His gifts are always from within. That divine gift of peace is established when love and faith become active. And in the great inner stillness the divine, superb peace is perfected.

When one reaches this point of peace he is no longer disturbed by any outside happenings. He remains unruffled, unaffected and undismayed by all outside confusion and turmoil. They never touch him.

In this peace, the gold that has been tried in the fires of his own soul, is completely stilled and purified so that it reflects only the pure image of his desires. This is rayed out to reflect the pattern of his thoughts into the great universal substance of "things hoped for." And that substance or material takes tangible form to fulfill every need, supply every want and fulfill every desire.

Anyone who has become so spiritualized he can use these divine powers of creation without having the image marred and distorted by greeds and evils and selfishness and discords has the gold that is completely purified. This is the gold that has been tried in the fires of his own soul. This is the real wealth. This is the power of creation as one learns to use it humbly, joyfully and in singing gratitude and eternal praise.

With this wealth always at hand one does not need to store up the corruptible treasures of earth.

This gold is the literal "pot of gold at the rainbow's end," described in *Secrets of Eternity*. This is the pure gold that is found when one can stand in the midst of his heartbreaks, amid the floods of the tempests of his life and lets the sun shine through the rain of his tears as a smile is called forth, in love and gratitude, to dispel the gloom and eradicate the threats of submersion. This is the power of eternal triumph over mortal disasters and storms as the spiritual gold reflects one's highest hopes and most noble aspirations and converts them into glorious realities. This is boundless wealth. This is power unlimited. This is God's power in action.

ALL THAT LOVE CONTAINS

Chapter XIII

Love is not a word. It is an essence! It is a power! It is a vibration! It is life!

Love is the most priceless element or tone in all existence. Rarium, uranium, platinum, gold and all the precious metals and jewels of the earth are but dross in comparison.

Love is a dynamic, living force. It is an eternal reality. It is the vehicle upon which the great Light is carried. It is the golden chariot that transcends time and eliminates space. It is spiritual. It is eternal. It is all-powerful.

As love is rayed out from a human heart it carries the Light of Christ with it to dispel the gloom and the darkness. It banishes evil and decay and misery. It overcomes fear. Negation cannot abide in its presence for love is a creative force of unlimited, unspeakable power.

Negative thoughts and vibrations are not creative. They are all defiling, contaminating and destructive. Love is not only a creative force, it is always constructive and beneficial. It can restore, rebuild and rectify. It can exalt and glorify.

It has been said that love is blind. Love is so exalted it does not even behold the scars and blemishes and ugliness which human sight gazes upon. Love looks deeper than the surface. It's healing tenderness penetrates all exteriors to enfold the very heart of substance and of people and

conditions and things. Love is not blind, love is only endowed with a deeper vision. Love looks beyond the visible
into the innermost depths of a man's soul and finds there
its resting place.

Man was created to be the bearer and the receptacle of
love even as a light globe was fashioned to be the container and dispenser of light.

Love is a balm that contains the powers of healing and
of renewing and of everlasting life within its effulgent
essence. Love is the great refiner and beautifier. Love is
more! Love is the key to every door. It is the creative
reality behind every righteous desire and every ardent hope.
Love is the cohesive power of the universe as it binds together atoms and substance. It holds families together—
the world and the entire universe. If love were withdrawn
all things would fall apart and disintegrate. When a human being eliminates love from his life he too begins to
fall apart. Love is not only eternal but it is the most desirable element to possess.

The Chinese adage portrayed by the three monkeys:
"Speak no evil; see no evil; hear no evil," is expressed in
negation. The true form, when confirmed by the outpouring power of love, is: "Speak only with the voice of love;
see only with the eyes of love; hear only with the ears
of love!"

When one develops his great God-given faculty of love
he will have the power to create and bring forth whatsoever his purified, spiritual vision of love beholds. He will
produce the divine harmonies his spiritually exalted ears
of love are trained to hear as those dynamic tones of creation are released right within his own heart. He will then
fulfill and accomplish whatsoever his love-inspired lips

may speak under the inspiration of his more exalted vision.

Like the Chinese proverb portrayed by the monkeys, most of man's works have been in reverse and in negation.

When man begins to open up the mind of his soul to contemplate the true wonders of his *existence* he will *stand forth* with all the powers of creation awaiting his command. Eternity itself will stand still before that divine command, "LET THERE BE—LIGHT!"

Yes! "Let there be Light!" If that is what you desire. Or let it be anything or any condition that will be for your own good and for the benefit of others.

"Let there be—Light" is the creative command of the soul as it asks for understanding. This is the superb command as the soul reaches out to take hold of the first element of Creation, that divine Christ Light and its companion element of love. "Let that Light of Christ, which is given to abide in every man who cometh into the world," be contacted and developed and brought forth in the full measure of ITS EXISTENCE! Let it STAND FORTH to fill your being as it is cradled and nurtured and released in love.

In and through love is the great Light developed. In love is it released. And by love the Light is fulfilled until one is filled full of Its glorifying, exalting essence of eternal comprehending, penetrating power of complete understanding that contains all knowledge as well as the gift of eternal life. Only in and through love can that inner Light be contacted and developed. The great Light is clothed in the exotic, unspeakable, wondrous garment of love. The Light is released and is carried forth on the very wings of love. Love is always the vehicle of Light.

This Light and its vehicle, love, have the power to dispel the darkness, transform the evils, overcome the fears and the doubts and the negation of this physical, mortal world. They have the power to exalt the individual who brings them forth into a higher realm of vibration and eternal triumphs as he takes hold of the creative powers of the universe.

Within the Light and the love, that must be developed within one's own being, are all powers held. "And all that the Father has is yours."

He who brings forth that Light until he is filled with Light shall comprehend all things for that Light is the power of understanding. It is quite necessary for one to be filled with this deeper understanding in order to take hold of those dynamic laws of creation to bring forth his righteous desires and to fulfill his own great destiny.

He who develops the divine gift of love will also bring forth that Christ Light and will thereby have the power to accomplish all things. It is quite impossible to perfect the gift of love without bringing forth the full out-pouring of that wondrous Light of Christ. And never is one complete without these two great powers of creation being brought to their fulfilment, or until the individual is fulfilled through them. When the song of inner thanks and gratitude is added to love and praise the Song of Creation is complete. "He who is thankful in all things shall be made glorious and the things of this earth shall be added unto him an hundred-fold; yea, more!"

The individual who begins to develop the divine gift of love will begin to change and will be transformed into a new, vibrant being of radiant personality endowed with poise and power. He will become increasingly attractive to his fellow beings as he automatically begins to attract others to him. They will seek to linger in the light he sheds forth. As he lets his light shine out, so that others beholding its effects will begin to glorify God by developing that same light within themselves, he will begin to render the greater service. There is no other way in which one can really glorify God except by bringing forth that Light in its full melody of love and praising gratitude. All the words of admonition, all the worldly anthems and all the sermons ever preached are but the symbolical shadows of this great reality—the Celestial Song of Creation released from a human heart.

As the love and the light are intermingled and brought forth, through praise and gratitude, nothing is impossible.

As one develops the pure, perfect gift of Christ's exalted, holy degree of love, so that it becomes the permanent factor in his life, old ideas begin to crumble, old thought patterns are erased and new, stupendous ones take their place. One's whole being begins to assume a new vitality, a new beauty and a new purpose and meaning.

In the gift of love, compassion replaces condemnation. Accusations melt away in an understanding comprehension of forgiveness. Mercy rays out its tenderness with a healing ray of restoring balm. As one's being is filled with this new tenderness the very cells of his body become imbued with it. The pores begin to breathe out this love until one becomes vibrantly radiant in a new, amazing beauty. One's hands ray out nothing but divine love and all things they touch are blessed thereby. One's eyes begin to express the pure love of God and there is nothing on this earth that is more beautiful. In this expanding, outpouring love the whole body is renewed and one becomes divine.

In this exalting, vibrating condition one speaks with

wisdom and with compassionate, understanding tenderness. And even his most gentle word will wing its way out to encompass the earth. Such a one need not confirm the truth of his statements by any oaths or added affirmations. They will *stand forth* more powerful than all the shouted words that could be trumpeted forth in strident, positive acclaim. His "yes" will mean *yes!* And his "No" will mean *no!* And he will never need to bear added witness to his statements by any oath of profanity or haranguement of argumentive verbosity.

Such a one will drip pearls from his lips as his phrases are released carrying healing in their tones. And comfort and the power of renewing and of radiant hope will flow out in the love-filled syllables of his most casual expression.

Love is the dynamic power of fulfilment. Love is the true reality behind creation. Love is the ethereal substance of existence! Love is the essence out of which each man's soul was formed!

As one develops the gift of love, hates and dislikes and jealousies and fears are banished. Love has the power to replace these negative monsters of the darkness without dismay, friction or searing battles. One has only to bring forth the love and the odious usurpers of man's mental and physical being flee and are gone.

Love is the heritage of every child of earth. Those who have permitted the evil, negative forces of darkness to replace love have become the victims of the errors and dismays and the anguished sufferings of the flesh and all the hates and discords and confusion they have fostered.

Man was created to subdue and master the earth and every condition and vibration upon it. Man has failed in his assignment simply because he has failed to bring forth the gift of perfect love. Earth has subdued man. It has beaten and betrayed him on every hand. It has triumphed over him and in the end it has swallowed up his remains. Man has failed because the negative forces of his mortal, physical nature have been given the power to rule and reign and so to destroy.

"Charity is the pure love of Christ, and it endureth forever; and whoso is found possessed of it at the last day, it shall be well with him. Wherefore my beloved brethren, *pray unto the Father with all the energy of heart,* that ye may be filled with this love, which He hath bestowed upon all who are true followers of His Son, Jesus Christ; that ye may become the sons of God; that when He shall appear we shall be like Him; for we shall see Him as He is; that we may have this hope; that we may be purified even as He is pure. Amen!"

Read and re-read the foregoing scripture until it is established in your mind to create its own pattern of thoughts and establish its own desires in your soul.

And now, let us open up our ears again to listen to the divinely inspired words of Paul upon the subject, remembering that "charity" is not alms-giving, as we now interpret it. The word has been so defiled by our modern interpretation its meaning has become not only corrupted but almost lost. We speak of charities as a means to salve our conscience and solve our civic obligations. We speak of "charity cases,"' with a belittling contempt even when we are employing a degree of compassion or seeking to render help.

The true meaning of the word "charity" as used by Paul was not "alms-giving." "Charity is the pure love of Christ!" In other words, "charity" is the pure, divine, Christ-like love!" It is the love that requires one to give a little of himself, in compassion and tenderness with an earnest blessing, along with whatever else he is able to part with.

"Though I speak with the tongues of men and of angels, and have not charity, I am become as sounding brass or a clanging cymbal.

"And though I have the gift of prophecy, and understand all mysteries, and all knowledge; and have all faith so that I could remove mountains, and have not charity (or the pure love of Christ), I am nothing.

"Charity suffereth long (without complaining or self-pity), and is kind; Charity envieth not (therefore knows no jealousy); charity vaunteth not itself (seeking always to excel and to hold the lime-light), is not puffed up (with pride).

"Doth not behave itself unseemingly, seeketh not her own (which is a low, earthly law—the law of gravity explained by Christine Mercie's book, Sons of God). Charity is not easily provoked, thinketh no evil (but thinketh only the most pure, beautiful things possible).

"Rejoices not in iniquity (or transgression), but rejoiceth in truth (which is the Light of Christ);

"Beareth all things, believeth all things (as it overcomes doubting), endureth all things (as it learns to be thankful in all things, thus transmuting them into blessings).

"Charity, (or the pure love of Christ), never faileth."

This pure, Christ-like love is each man's own key to divinity.

"The love of God that is shed forth through the hearts of the children of men is the Fruit of the Tree of Life!" But this love is only shed forth through one's heart in its fulness as man prays for it with all the energy of his heart

and seeks with all his strength and understanding to develop the most sacred, divine gift of love so that it rules
his life.

As man begins to comprehend the power and the marvel
and the wonder of the dynamic gift of love and to desire
it, so that he makes an effort to develop it, he will com·
mence the great work of his own completion. He will step
forth to fulfill the role of his own exaltation as he begins
not only to bring forth that holy gift but the divine Seed
of God that is contained within that love. The holy Spark
or Seed of God Himself is held in an embryonic form
within each and every man. As love is perfected that Seed
is developed. Then it is that one is born of love, or of
God, as St. John so beautifully explains in his epistles.
The holy, immaculate conception is already established.
When God conceived man at the dawn of creation He
placed the divine Seed or spark of Himself within the
innermost soul of every child.

As love is developed and brought forth that divine Seed
is also developed and brought forth until it fills the mortal
tabernacle of man. When it is fully matured until it fills
one's entire being he will be "Filled with the fulness of
God!"

As love triumphs the eternal victory of man's fulfilment
is completed and accomplished.

These great truths that are now being revealed to you
have been hidden down the centuries. Love that kingdom
within, that inner realm of your own soul. Love that sacred
realm of the great Christ Light and the abode of His great
love. And love above all that divine Seed of God Himself,
that immaculate conception of Deity contained within you.
Love that inner realm and that Sacred Seed of God as you

would love a little child. Hold it in your thoughts and become increasingly aware of Its presence. Enfold it ever in your protecting love as you learn to shield it from darkness and fears and the destructiveness of your own doubting and the vibrations of your mortal, negative thoughts and feelings and it "will grow and wax strong." As it is completed you will truly be born of God—an immortal son of the most High, with all that the Father has fulfilled in you.

Man has spent his time and his energies in seeking for precious minerals and metals and priceless jewels and the buried, hidden treasures contained within the earth. Yet the most priceless jewel of all is the Seed of God held embryoed within man himself. This jewel of jewels is enfolded in the divine love of God that is held deep within a man's own soul. This Seed must be nurtured through "the great Christ Light that is given to abide in every man who cometh into the world." This Spark of God is awakened, or quickened by the release of that Light from within and the development of the sacred gift of love. This treasure of treasures is brought forth only through man's own expanding love and through his increasing awareness of Light.

This most priceless treasure, contained within the sacred element of eternal love and enfolded in the essence of Christ's own Light, is every individual's who will only be-live and bring it forth from its tomb. And henceforth the way to bring it forth is also yours—the Way Christ marked—the Way He trod.

Be humble in your great discovery of these sacred, eternal truths. And be tenderly grateful in your labors of delivery. The way is yours and the treasure is your own.

Remember always that "Eye hath not seen, nor ear heard,

neither hath it entered into the heart of man, the things God hath prepared for them that love Him." Only a dim glimpse of the powers that will be yours, as you develop this great love for God, is given here. As you cast from you all doubting and begin to bring forth His Light and develop the great love you will be filled with the understanding that will fulfill all things.

THE LOST CHORD

Chapter XIV

A voice of longing cries out of every human soul in moments of unforgettable loneliness. It is a voice that is felt, not heard. In some it is released through the haunting strains of music. Others hear it through the flaming colors of a sunset or the awakening splendor of a dawn. And there are those who are most aware of it while shouldering their way through crowded throngs. Some sense it in the vibrating rhythm of the ocean waves, or in the vastness of a rolling sea. Some are gripped in the loneliness of that wailing, inner echo as they gaze upward into a star-flung sky. Some hear it in the softness of filtered moonlight as it melts into the shadows of the trees. Others may hear it as they gaze upon the heavenly expanse of misty, floating clouds, or in a flower-spangled meadow, or a blooming orchard, or from some lofty mountain peak, or in the silent heart of a rose.

None have ever lived who have not felt the haunting refrain of that "Lost Chord" moaning out its unforgettable echo of lamentation as it sighed forth its desolating loneliness at some moment or other in their lives. And there are those who hear it often as they *yearn intensely for— they know not what.* And one and all try to silence that haunting plaint as it sobs forth its heartbreaking burden of uncomprehended sorrows from some long forgotten memory—or world—or lost existence?

That lonely moan was my cradle song. It was the only music of my childhood as it was picked up and re-echoed by the winds wailing across the drab, sage-covered hills. I would not escape the lonely, forlorn, melancholy chant of forsakenness and desolating pain that seemed to expand until my whole life was filled with the hurt of its despairing sadness.

And for that I am most grateful!

I had no choice but to listen. There was no way for me to elude the desolating echo of those unrecorded tones as they played their lonely dirge upon the fibres of my being. And so it was I learned the lamentation of the soul's despairs. I began to comprehend the meaning of those wailing tones as I struggled to master them. And in my experiments I rearranged the sequence of each note as I played the complete refrain in breathtaking reverse. It was in my rearrangement I discovered the great "Lost Chord" and the powers it contains and the unutterable glory of its true rendition. All that is necessary in order to change that lonely chant into an exquisite harmony of infinite power is to express the same tones in praise and love and gratitude. Then the strange "Lost Chord" becomes a symphony of unutterable beauty—which is no longer "lost" within a man's mortal being. It becomes a triumphant masterpiece of dynamic harmonious accord.

That lonely, melancholy chant of sadness, echoing, unbidden out of each man's soul, is but the unfulfilled, unexpressed, scrambled tones of the great "Lost Chord," as they are released without skill or understanding. It is like the exquisite notes of a masterpiece being tossed forth at random without harmony or reason directing them. The notes may all be there but there is no lovely melody expressed, only tones of sad inharmony.

The "Lost Chord," in its correct rendition contains the wondrous tones of creation. The "Lost Chord" embraces the vibrations of love and praise and gratitude in their most powerful, dynamic intensity. In the soul's lament of dismay this superb masterpiece of power is played in reverse. The triumphant symphony of Creative glory is played backward through the mortal instrument of man. In this negative release it becomes a refrain of desolating loneliness, the reverted expression of a sad, thwarted soul.

Within the three major tones of love and praise and gratitude are held a hundred little rills of glee and happiness and singing, joyous accomplishments.

That lonely cry of the human heart is the melody of creation being expressed in its negative form as it is released with an empty echo of forgotten meaning and lost powers. Yet within that lonely, unforgettable, inner lament is held the powers of creation and the keys of fulfilment when understood. The notes need only to be rearranged. In that yearning, inner cry the tones of the "Lost Chord" will be heard if only the music is transposed. That inverted song of triumphant fulfilment and everlasting power becomes a plaintive wail of the soul's frustrating despair when its reversion is permitted to go forth unmastered.

The "Lost Chord" holds no sadness, loneliness, or forlorn, melancholy reproach of longing ache and searing desolation when man's consciousness takes hold of it and turns its notes around. Then it becomes the sublime, wondrous symphony of creative glory.

The "Lost Chord" of creative power and fulfilment contains the three major over-tones of love and praise and singing gratitude. As stated before, within each of these three dynamic tones is enfolded an independent melody of sublime, exquisite, exalting power. Within this dynamic "Lost Chord" are the full powers of creation contained. That "Lost Chord" has only been lost within the physical nature of man.

Now, to analyze more fully the splendor and the power contained within that famed "Lost Chord," that you might become the master of it, or the dynamic expressor of the Symphony of Creation and its three major tones, each measure must be more thoroughly explained, in order that these prodigious powers might be placed within your hands.

Gratitude contains the eternal law of increase, the complete power of divine multiplication. All blessings are increased when placed within the powerful vibrations of sincere thanksgiving. All the spiritual powers of plenty and increase are contained within the unutterable glory of that singing gratitude when released from a thankful human heart. The prayer of thanksgiving is the law of plenty as it swings into activity. Through deep gratitude the fulness of supply begins to be discharged in increasing abundance to more than fill the measure of one's needs.

Gratitude is an essential vibrating part of the everlasting glory of creation as it is released to play its own part in the great symphony of the Universe—the Creative Song of Fulfilment—the triumphant New Song of all power.

It is a simple matter to master this dynamic vibration of everlasting glory and power and so prove its immeasurable worth. One cannot prove its powers just by reading this record and agreeing with it any more than one can become a musician by enjoying the performance of an orchestra.

One must practice sending out those divine rays of gratitude right within himself as he works to master the greatest of all harmonies. One must play it upon his own being until it becomes a singing part of every thought. It must become a heart-felt reaction to every happening, a song of release for every minor gift and blessing, regardless how small. Only the gift of appreciation fully releases the power of gratitude's exquisite tones of stupendous glory.

In the mastery and release of this great power of gratitude one must lift his vision completely above his lacks and even his possible destitute circumstances. He must not look at the things he does not have, nor concentrate his vision upon his deficiencies. He must lift his eyes to behold the things he does possess and give praise and thanks for them. The gratitude must issue out from the innermost center of his soul for every tiny gift and blessing. He must learn to rejoice in every meager comfort and for every mouthful of food. He must be thankful for every necessary holding entrusted to him to take care of his needs. As he gives thanks he will soon begin to receive the benefit of luxuries. And if he will but continue in this release of heart-felt gratitude all his physical wants will be supplied and the spiritual ones will follow. He will automatically grow into the richer blessings of divine fulfilment.

"He who is thankful in all things shall be made glorious; and the things of this earth shall be added unto him an hundredfold; yea, more!"

The prayer of thanksgiving contains the law of plenty.

If one only has a crust of bread it can be increased into a loaf. Perhaps not instantly. But it can be. This is the same law Christ used in feeding the multitude. It is the law Elisha instructed the widow to use in increasing the supply from her small cruse of oil to take care of all her needs and purchase her freedom and the freedom of her sons and then leave her with an over-abundance. According to one's perfecting of its use will be the measure of time required to fulfill the law of supply in all its completeness. It will begin to work immediately for any who will exercise its powers, though perhaps not in its fulness. But as one continues to use and practice the law it becomes powerful and, in time, instantaneous. The law can work in an instant if you will master its full technique. The time element will be according to your own faith as you learn to perfect and use the law within your own being. As you begin to live by this higher law you will soon KNOW of its powers and be able to use them freely and fully.

The law of increase is a living, eternal law and more unfailing and more powerful than the law of planting and harvest.

Suppose you only have a dollar—or even a dime to your name. Use the coin for your needs with singing gratitude as you release it with joy and thanksgiving that must come from deep within the heart. When this law is used perfectly there can be no worried glances cast toward tomorrow as you invite its fears to take over and to rule. The great, glorious song of gratitude and true thankfulness must hold the vibrations of your being so high that you can take no thought for tomorrow.

As you continue to use this great, unfailing law of gratitude you will establish the supply to furnish your most urgent needs. If it was a dollar you sent out with your blessing of thanks accompanying it, and it is increased "an hundred-fold," you may complain that a hundred dollars, in this day, is not very much. That is true. But as you continue to use the law with that hundred dollars they can be increased by a hundred-fold or the equivalent thereof until your blessings are all multiplied in conformity to your own understanding. The law is eternal and the supply from which it draws is unending.

This law of gratitude is a divine reality and an everlasting power. But each individual must make use of it for himself. It cannot be fulfilled by a slack, hap-hazard, lackadaisical method. It must be worked with earnestness and intensity until it becomes absolute knowledge advanced into power. When this law is used there can be no curse upon one's possessions for one will have taken God into partnership with him in his every venture. And God Himself will supply the increase until there will not be room enough to receive it. No man ever needs to cheat his fellowmen in order to gain the comforts and luxuries he desires. He has only to fulfill the higher law and all things will be added unto him.

As one works, or lives this law of supply and increase and fulfills it with joyous, understanding persistence it will become a vibrating reality issuing forth from his own soul at all times.

Love is another measure from the "Lost Chord" of Creation. Love is the law of transmutation. Love can so exalt and transform every adverse condition and the individual expressing it that they take on immortality. Every individual who perfects the symphony of love will be lifted into a vibration of triumphant loveliness and beauty. Love is the law that can lift one from a mediocre individual into a master. Love conquers the negative conditions of one's nature as well as of his exterior world. Love transforms the powers of darkness as it converts their energies into the creative rays of powerful, glorious, exalted existence. Love changes doubts and fears into living, vibrant faith with all its powers of complete fulfilment.

Love's power is unspeakable when it is intelligently used and continuously exercised. It can accomplish the impossible. Within the power of love is contained all joy and all happiness and all perfection. No one can possibly become "hide-bound" or sealed in orthodoxed self-righteousness or bigotry or become a repulsive or domineering person, or a failure who develops love.

Love is the outpouring energies of the soul that perfects the gift of faith and then releases it in its limitless capacity to perform the "greater works." Love perfects the obedience that yields all personal desires to the Will of God and so blends the individual into the pattern of his own divine fulfilment. Love is the purifier. Love fulfills all the laws as it is enhanced and completed by gratitude and praise. Love, in its fulness, will transform every living soul, who perfects it, into a child of light, endowed with gracious poise and majestic power.

Love must be practiced constantly, not in words, for words cannot carry the glory of its divine reality in their empty sounds. Love must be *exercised* as one would practice in order to become a great musician. He must open his heart to permit love to flow out as he sends it forth to enfold the world. The fountains of love increase as love flows forth. Love contains the full power of healing and of renewing. Love is of God and it is truly "The Fruit of the Tree of Life as it is shed forth through the hearts of the children of men!"

Praise, the third dynamic measure in the famed "Lost

Chord," contains the law of fulfilment. Praise releases the vibrations that complete and fulfill all things and all conditions and the individual who lifts his heart in joyous, singing praise. It is the triumphant "Hosannas" shout of old—the exulting shout of glory! It is the complete acknowledgement of God! It is the tones of singing, creative fulfilment in their fullest measure of release! Praise is that *"Glory to God!"* vibration that is sent forth from an overflowing heart, bursting with joy!

That "New Song, which none can learn but the righteous," contain these three dynamic vibrations expressed in their fulness. This is the dynamic Song of Creation! It is the Celestial Symphony of the Universe! It is the heavenly "Lost Chord" of all power! Praise and love and gratitude are the major over-tones of that divine, exulting anthem of eternal triumph. And surely none but the righteous can master it. But he who does master it will assuredly become righteous. These released tones are the transforming, exalting, fulfilling tones of creation. Master them and you will become a master.

Remember: Gratitude is the law of increase and multiplication. Love is the law of transmutation as it transforms conditions and things. It has the power to translate the individuals who perfect it into a higher order of existence. And Praise is the law of completion and of divine fulfilment. It is the "Hosannas" shout of victory, in Glory to God!

Combine these three major vibrations of praise and love and gratitude into a symphony of exulting glory as they are released from your heart, instead of from your lips. The tongue has no power to express these great vibrations, except when the heart so overflows the lips must cry aloud.

If they did not the very stones would be called upon to release the vibrancy of their unrestrainable power.

As one masters the divine Symphony of Creation he will have the power to *step forth* into the realms of supreme achievement. Then it is that one is fulfilled—or "filled with the fulness of God!"

This New Song must be continuously expressed as it is released from the individual in vibrations of exalting glory until he becomes a very part of it. "For he who can interpret the wonders of the Lord will be dissolved and will become that which is interpreted." This "New Song" must wing its way out on the joyous releasing from human hearts until it conquers the darkness and overcomes the fears and the lacks and the discords and the dismays and transforms them into the boundless powers of full achievement.

Each individual who desires to participate in the "greater works" must become a greater musician as he masters every note and tone of the sublime Symphony of Creation—the Celestial Song of the Universe—The New Song of dynamic, unutterable power. He must be able to express its tones so perfectly not one vibration of negation can ever again touch him. No fear or doubt or confusion must ever be permitted to sound forth their discords of destructive disintegration within his being. The soul must *stand forth* in its full majesty to sing the dynamic anthem of creative glory in the fulness of its divine power of Celestial fulfilling.

This divine Symphony of Creation, held within those three major tones of that sublime "Lost Chord," contain the complete law of levitation, as explained in Christine Mercie's booklet, SONS OF GOD. As this Song of Creation becomes the reverberating, stupendous vibration, released from within the individual so that no discordant, negative notes can possibly enter or be released through his being, with their deteriorating destructiveness, one truly overcomes the earth-binding law of gravity and mortal limitations.

In the book, SECRETS OF ETERNITY, the three great rays are designated as colors and are described as being the Christ rays. These three major colors are known to be the foundation colors from which all others are formed. These rays are living vibration——the vibrations of creation as viewed by spiritual eyes. These same vibrations are the great tones of the "Lost Chord" when heard by the ears that have been exalted into their fullest functioning.

Vibrations are the true reality behind creation and all existence.

Gratitude, when released from a singing, grateful heart, is a vibration of limitless power. It is visible to spiritualized eyes as the ruby-red ray of Jesus Christ, Son of the Living God! It is the ray of courage and acceptance and increase.

Praise releases the golden ray of glory—the vibration of triumphant overcoming as it fulfills all things.

The third, major ray, is the divine, exquisite blue ray of Christ. It is impossible to describe the vivid aliveness of this transcending color of divine glory. It is beautiful beyond words or human utterance. It is known as the Christ ray of "Faith", or love in its fullest expression. This ray is brought forth by the individual's power to believe or to *be* and *live* according to his highest hopes and purest vision. As one *be-lives* the higher teachings he develops the dynamic blue ray of *faith*. This divine, blue ray of faith holds within it the keys of absolute *knowing*. And "Knowledge is power!" This is the power needed to transform all the ugly, sordid conditions of life into beauty and loveliness and to translate a man from a mortal creature of weaknesses and ills into a being arrayed in the powerful vibrations of everlasting Light.

These rays are vibrations that are released from within a man as the pure Christ Light is brought forth from within. These three major vibrations hold the entire spectrum of living colors within their holy embrace. These are the three major colors from which all the other shades and tones and hues are formed. These are the living vibrations of limitless power when released from within man.

These rays, when sent forth knowingly, are unlimited. They ascend to the throne of God instantly. There is no power in existence that can retard them, hold them back, dim or deflect them in their course. They create and hold open the channels along which God's blessings flow back from the throne of All-fulfilment. They are the opened windows of heaven through which stream forth man's blessings. And these blessings continue to increase and to multiply as long as the channels are held open. They continue to enlarge until there is not room enough to contain the wonders of their supply.

These three rays are the channels along which the answers to your own prayers will come. Open those channels and you will walk with God.

These three major colors or rays are but the vibrations of that divine Christ Light as It is released in Its fullest measure from the heart of man. Within these rays is held the completed glory of the full spectrum in every glorified hue and color.

These same released vibrations are also the tones of sound of which this record speaks. These three major tones of the divine "Lost Chord" hold within their vibrant release every note of purity and beauty and the full exulting joy of the soul as they wing their way forth from an overflowing human heart!

Gratitude and praise and love, that is expressed in the complete belief of living, powerful faith, are the three Christ rays of vibrating, everlasting power. They are the three major tones of the dynamic Symphony and are known as the Christ keys of Creation. Within their holy scope is held the Celestial Song of the Universe! The dynamic, fulfilling, triumphant symphony of breathtaking power! The entire force of Creation! The New Song!

These three major tones have been known as the "Lost Chord" because they have been lost within the physical being of man. In his awakening they will be released to open the doors to new, spiritual worlds as man advances into the complete fulfilment of himself.

"For it is given to abide in you, the record of heaven, the Comforter, the truth of all things; that which quickeneth all things, and maketh alive all things; that which knoweth all things, and hath all power!"

Yes, these things and these powers have been given to abide in man but man has permitted them to become lost and so has remained unfulfilled. And so it is that from within his own being comes that lonely, haunting cry of mourning.

To the eyes that have become spiritualized these vibrations appear as colors. To the ears that have been trained to hear, they are heard as the vibrant tones of living sound—even the Song of Creation!

They are the same vibrations whether registered upon the eyes or upon the ears or upon the whole wondrous being of man. They are the dynamic vibrations upon which the Universe was laid. They are the vibrations by which it is maintained. They are the vibration of creation.

These three major vibrations and all related ones are expressed both in color and in sound and in the invisible powers of eternity.

When man is completely spiritualized he passes beyond the five mortal senses and instead of gaining information through his eyes and his ears and his nostrils and taste and touch he gains his knowledge with a complete awareness of full comprehension. Then it is that all the physical senses are united with the spiritual ones into the full, dynamic instrument of All-knowing.

Yes, "all that the Father has is yours" to use and to fulfill!

LIFE ETERNAL!

Chapter XV

"Let the dead bury their dead!" So advised Jesus. But the world has never understood how very literal those words are.

The majority of mankind have so yielded themselves to the powers of death it is almost as though death had already claimed them. These half-dead ones, without the enlivening vibrations of the tingling life force active within, have nothing really better to do than to attend death. Many of them have already enshrined and glorified death as they await the touch of his hand upon them.

And there are those who have made dismal, dreary little shrines of themselves, dedicated to death, as they mope listlessly through life——expecting to be compensated in a great, glorious HERE-AFTER for either their imagined ills or actual ones. Those who never attempt to overcome one negative vicissitude or to rise above any trial, misfortune or disappointment, have no claim upon glory. They have permitted themselves to be "overcome" instead of exerting their great God-given mandate in triumphant "overcoming."

And there are those who unwittingly invite death into their homes as a permanent guest. He sits at their tables with them, walks at their heels, waits beside their beds, sometime for years, as they nurse some physical handicap

in weak self-pity. Their greatest sorrow is that others do
not sit down and mourn with them over *their* CONDITION
as they linger by their imagined graves in grieving antici-
pation. These are truly the chief mourners at their own
funerals.

These have worshipped death and evil and darkness
though they expect God to exalt them into the highest
heaven in "The Great Beyond." Their invitation to death
will be answered soon enough without the welcome mat
and the spread banquet table. Such have no other goal
and are drawn irrevocably toward that dismal, back door
of death. They believe that death holds the keys of their
release from every ill. And how can they possibly know
that their established mental habits go with them, unless
they seek to understand? Their cultivated taste for misery
has become so savory to their minds they actually relish
the anguished, negative conditions they have fostered upon
themselves. These attitudes and habits and cultivated misfortunes go with them into the grave—and beyond. They
are their own. They have become a very part of their fibre
and their existence. These unfortunate ones have held to
every hurt, every sorrow, every misfortune and every hate,
refusing mentally to relinquish one single disagreeable
happening or condition. Their good is forgotten and crowded
out until only the evil is remembered—and so remains.
They do not realize that it is more natural and much easier
to eliminate the evil by glorifying the good, with that inner song of gratitude and joy, than it is to develop the evil.

"Joy is of the Saints. And *none can put it on* but they
alone." Joy is actually something one "puts on" like a robe
of glory as he overcomes the darkness, the despairs, the
negative conditions of earth—and finally conquers death

itself. True Joy is a highly spiritual quality and the very developing of it will make one a *Saint*.

Why worship death or yearn for its release?
Why think that death can make your toubles cease
While you lack courage to even face your foes
As you yield weakly to the slightest wind that blows?
Why seek to escape in vault or silent crypt,
Giving death the pow'r to write your mortal script?

Gird up your loins and tell me, if you can,
Were you born to be a coward, or a man?
If you're a man then pray, *"God's Will* be done!"
And know His Will is that *man overcome!*

Strip death of his scythe and black, dismal robe
As your soul is roused to "ask and seek" and probe.
Then will you know that death can have no claim
On those who glorify the Light and it alone acclaim.
For they overcome life's darkness and its strife
As they overcome life's darkness and its strife
In praise and love and singing gratitude—
The Celestial Symphony—their great beatitude.

Those who constantly seek the blank void of inebriation or who crawl into their little cells and crevices or darkened, dreary rooms are seeking to escape life by embracing death and all that it represents. They love the darkness more than they love the light.

These too are the dead who are attending death as life is gradually forced out and they succumb to all the evils they have permitted into their daily living.

In the Lost Books of the Bible, that have been found, and translated is this precious information given by Nicodemus in his eighteenth chapter and twelfth verse: *"O Satan, Prince of all evil,* AUTHOR OF DEATH, *and source of all pride . . "*, etc.

God did not ordain nor create death. Lucifer did. God only permitted it. He will continue to permit it until man himself accepts the Higher Way.

"We consider that God has created man with a mind capable of instruction, and a faculty which may be enlarged in proportion to the heed and diligence given to the light communicated from heaven to the intellect; and that the nearer man approaches perfection the clearer are his views, and the greater his enjoyments, till he has overcome the evils of his life and lost every desire for sin; and like the ancients, arrives at the point of faith where he is wrapped in the power and glory of his Maker and is caught up to dwell with him."

So this question must be asked: How can anyone possibly partake of the "Life more abundant" who does not have a deep reverence and a true appreciation for that most holy, divine gift of Life? One must appreciate his own sacred life as well as respect the gift in his fellowmen in order to receive of its abundance.

One must be ever aware of the vibrancy of that surging life force right within himself in order to receive of its fulness and its breathtaking powers. This sacred gift of life is the true reality of existence. It is the caressing, nurturing, enfolding benediction of Almighty God manifesting in the individual. It is the very truth and substance of being. It is the power and the love of our divine Sire flowing from within.

It is the everlasting plan of God that each individual partake of the gift of life fully or in its complete fulness. This is the "Life more abundant!" When one partakes of the gift of life in its fulness and abundance he is no longer a drab, dull, impotent mortal. He becomes a dynamic being aflame with purpose and power.

This sacred "Life more abundant" is merely the regular gift of life developed and brought forth into the highest potency as one becomes completely aware of it. It is the full establishment of vibrancy and joy and vivid, glorious, purposeful living. The principle of life is increased and expanded into its divine powers by the ecstasy of appreciation. Only in gratitude and joy and understanding can it become fully established.

"If a man hate his life, he shall find it," means that if one is dissatisfied and discontented with his meager, skimpy, desolate, little mortal existence then, if he uses his perogative aright, he can reach out into the greater LIFE and bring it forth. Thus it is possible to take hold of the "Life more abundant!" This "Life more abundant" is the gift of life in its fulness ás the physical, mortal elements become embued with the full, surging vibration of the great spiritual force of LIFE in all Its dynamic, everlasting power. And he who takes hold of it fully need never die. This is the law.

Death comes because the individual himself relinquishes the gift of life. He permits the life force to be crowded out by his own tired, resentful, self-pitying thoughts; his negative attitudes or his degenerate desires and lust-filled, greedy actions. Every dreary, evil, hate-filled, jealous thought; every sensual, lustful thought and act; every discordant, negative word and attitude are but the destructive forces of death bombarding the life of man. Every evil vibration that is permitted to abide within the being of man contains the destroying, pushing, shoving forces of conquest as they battle against the glorious gift of LIFE. As man himself sits by and permits these evil forces of darkness to operate within him the life principle is gradually crowded out and defeated by man's ignorance and his unconscious willingness.

As any individual harbors his ordinary, everyday, mortal attitudes, he is operating on the physical level of existence. He is not only inviting the forces of death to proceed in their softening, undermining "cold war", he is assisting them to carry on in their slow, subtle procedure of destruction. Man himself may be only the neutral ground on which the forces of life and death wage their silent, ingenious war. But that war is for the man himself. His very LIFE is at stake. And the victory or the defeat is his own as death triumphs in the end or the man himself takes a hand in the struggle and "overcomes."

Man has stood indifferently, ignorantly by and permitted himself to be the unholy habitation of all that will eventually destroy him unless he begins to exert himself and direct the raging battle of thoughts and emotions that arise continually from within—or that are hurled at him from without. Man has the right to direct the battle and to reap the victory. Yet man has rarely exerted his divine nature and privilege of choice because he has not realized that the battle is truly his own.

The gift of life is exalted and increased through the joy of right thinking and the positive force of right actions. Life itself becomes victorious and completely established through a triumphant awareness of inner rejoicing as the individual learns to appreciate Its dynamic glory of ever-lasting power.

"The Life more abundant" is the vibrant, singing, wondrous potency of complete existence. It is the triumphant, powerful reality of *being*. It is the melodious awareness of the eternal power of God in its fullest expression.

As one takes hold of the most holy gift of life, with his awakening faculty of understanding appreciation, he receives the "Life more abundant!" The life force increases continually within him instead of diminishing. As that life force is comprehended and established one naturally grows into the "Life more abundant." As this sacred Life force increases old age and physical deterioration ends. They are conquered as the cells of the body are spiritualized and hence released from death. This is the "overcoming" or the vanquishing of all mortal ills. And when the "life more abundant" is completely established death is automatically conquered.

Death itself begins with the cells and the tissues as they are gradually undermined and destroyed by the vibrations of all negative, evil thoughts and fears. Death begins its battle from the day one is born. It is carried on through the emotions and the thoughts and the words and the acts of the individual as he matures and is trained to act and to re-act, perhaps violently, to every circumstance and condition of life which does not please him.

Man has never fully understood the truth of God's word, given in the very beginning of time, when He relinquished unto His children the dominion of the earth. Man was, in that day, given full dominion over himself also. He was given the right to choose and to select and to control his own thoughts and actions and re-actions and the unspeakable power of vibrations he would release through his own being. He was also given the power to control and to rule over the vibrations that sought to enter his being from without. The kingdom and dominion is entirely his own. If he has permitted the robbers and usurpers to enter his kingdom and take control then he suffers through his own acquiescent surrender.

To learn to appreciate that most holy gift of life, centered right within oneself, is to learn to appreciate the power and the dominion of God in its unutterable wholeness of expression.

Glory in the gift of life! Rejoice in it! Praise God for it and watch it unfold in the beauty and power of its sublime fulfilment—even into the "Life more abundant." Then lift your eyes to behold the wonder and exquisite beauty of that gift of life within your fellowmen. Look beyond the fleshy tomb in which it is concealed. Look into the sublime gift Itself and you will behold the majesty and the power of God in operation. Let your mind reach out to contemplate It in reverent tenderness in the being of every living soul and you will help to bring it forth in them.

Go another step and rejoice in that superb gift of life in every growing thing, in every flowing stream, in every blooming flower and singing bird and in the breathtaking expanse of the heavens as you behold "the stars move upon their wings in their glory in the midst of the power of God."

Rejoice in the sacred gift of life as your heart expands in gratitude and you will feel the life force begin to surge anew within the members of your own being.

In the singing song of ecstasy and the vibrant gratitude

of heart-felt praise, life is increased and established and the body becomes quickened and renewed.

As long as there is breath and intelligence LIFE is always there awaiting man's acceptance of It in Its complete fulness. Love the life God has given you and watch it unfold into beauty and loveliness and power. Love is like sunshine to that divine, precious gift of Life. Through tender, understanding appreciation it can be brought forth until one becomes the powerful ruler of his inner domain and the master of his destiny.

The gift of Life is increased through joy. If flourishes in happiness and is established in gentle tenderness and singing glory. It is the one eternal reality of existence. It IS existence in all Its completeness and fulness. It is health! It is joyous ecstasy! It is an abundance of all that is good and beautiful and worthwhile.

In the vibrant gift of life one is exalted above the dreary, mediocre phase of drab, ugly, mortal existence. Life is the expression of vibrancy and joy and perfection. It is always beautiful! Life is that wonderful "Glory to God" vibration that unfailingly exalts one into that realm of *abundant Life* as It becomes manifest in man through his own understanding.

Life is the great eternal! It is your own in some degree, just as you stand. It can be yours in its fullest measure as you open your heart and mind and soul to receive It. It can even be yours in Its fulness, if you desire It. It can be more! It can become you if so be you glorify It right within yourself.

That "Life more abundant" is that million-dollar vibration! It is more. It is a vibration beyond price or physical purchasing power. That vibration of glory, which is *Life*

in expression, is the "White raiment." In that highest vibration of joyous ecstasy and singing, inner praise one
clothes himself in the holy vibration of Light. It is time
that man realizes that the "white raiment", which all are
instructed to clothe themselves in, is pure spiritual substance.
It is the glorious substance of heaven. It is vibration in its
highest potency of beauty and creative power. Vibration
is the material or substance of the higher realms. Vibration
is the spiritual "substance of things hoped for" as they are
gathered into form by the life force of creation.

Every man is clothed in the vibrations of his own thoughts
and mental habits.

When one's vibrations are exalted by joyous praise and
loving thoughts, that are held triumphantly above *doubts*,
he is taking hold of the eternal substance of heaven. This
substance will fulfill his own righteous desires for it is the
very element out of which the "things hoped for" are
created. By comprehending the use and the power of this
element or substance a man can glorify his life and will
be able to clothe himself in the "White raiment," which
no darkness or evil can touch or defile. "Faith is the substance of things hoped for." It is the material or element
out of which the "White raiment" is woven and out of
which all good is created. It is the vibration of Life expressing in Its great creative potency. Faith is a vibration
which man can use at all times. It is an element of power
and is more real than any substance of mortality.

In that wondrous "White raiment" of glorified vibrations and exalted praise and adoration one becomes clothed
in the spiritual substance that covers the shame of his physical, mortal nakedness. He actually becomes robed in Christ's
Light. This white apparel is the substance or material of

Light as It is released from within man. This Light is vibration. It is the vibration or element of Faith. It is an actual element of life itself.

This true vibration of creation clothes the individual as it exalts and glorifies him. It banishes all lacks and fulfills all things—even the man himself. In It nothing is lacking and no destitute or unhappy condition can possibly exist.

The "glory to God" vibration of LIFE and hence FAITH is expressed and developed in that inner song of triumphant, glorious gratitude and exulting praise. It is contacted and' released from a full heart of thanksgiving as one reaches beyond words and thoughts into the depths of his own soul where the powers of God are contacted and released. As one makes this contact, through praise and love and gratitude, the creative song of the universe is released in its powers of perfect manifestation.

That holy gift of "Life more abundant" is the reality of being in its entirety as one is completely filled with "The Spirit of the Lord" or the divine "Light of Christ." That effulgent vibration of "Life more abundant" is contacted and released from within as the Christ Light is brought forth in joyous love and deepest gratitude. Then faith is perfected. It could even be stated that the Light of Christ is contacted and brought forth when the full appreciation of the divine gift of Life is accepted and brought forth through love and glory.

That exalted, wondrous vibration of sublime glory IS the "Life more abundant" as belief advances into the stage of assured, positive faith. And this positive faith always carries with it the seed or capacity of KNOWING. And "knowledge is power!" It is as one begins to use his knowledge of the higher laws that the greater works are accomplished.

No man was ever created who was not entitled to the "Life more abundant, even Life eternal" if he will but reach forth his hand and lay claim to the gift by fulfilling Its laws of singing glory. The gift is your own. It has been waiting from the very beginning for you to accept it.

It is only an appreciation of that most holy, divine, stupendous gift of LIFE that can establish It permanently and powerfully within an individual.

LIFE! "LIFE MORE ABUNDANT! EVEN LIFE ETERNAL!" The second is but a fuller manifestation of the first. The third, or the Life eternal is but the first and second developed into its supreme power and excellence. One's own meager little mortal life, or whatsoever degree he may possess of it can be developed and glorified until the second and third phases are fully established. One may be expressing only a weak, resentful little shred of life as he permits it to be beaten by every vicissitude and vibration of fear and despair and ugliness or wrath. Or one may have enough vitality expressing to fulfill a mortal existence of physical satisfaction on the earth level, if that is all he is willing to express. The individual is the one who makes the bargain with life whether he will accept the penny's worth or require the fullest amount of the most glorious abundance of fulfilment and power.

Life, in its fullest magnitude, is always awaiting man's comprehension, appreciation and acceptance of It.

The gift of Life is God's own power in action. Life is always active, progressive, expanding and gloriously beautiful. Life is never ugly nor static nor disagreeable. Man himself may express his life in these terms. That is up to him. But it is entirely within each individual to decide how he will express his gift of life. It can be expressed for good—or for evil. If one uses It to express the evil, then it becomes evil to him and he dies by the sword of its destructive force. It is a two-edged sword and the individual reaps whatsoever he manifests in his own life.

The gift of Life itself is a vibration of singing, triumphant glory, even the very power of God in action. It can be increased within one until he is re-vitalized and his whole existence becomes glorified and exalted. This "Life more abundant" can only be expressed through him who is completely aware of It.

"Therefore it is given to abide in you: the record of heaven; the Comforter; the peaceable things of immortal glory; the truth of all things; that which quickeneth all things, which maketh alive all things; that which knoweth all things, and hath all power, according to wisdom, mercy, justice and judgment." Or according to the irrevocable, eternal law of God. And it is up to man to bring these powers of LIFE forth and use them.

As one learns to take hold of those ecstatic moments of high inspiration he can gradually establish them permanently through his own awakening desires for righteousness. These high moments of joy are the spiritual realities and are increased through tender thoughts of loveliness and compassion and joyous gratitude. As one's thoughts are trained to encompass and enfold only goodness and mercy and love, he begins to assert his dominion over the mortal kingdom of himself, which God entrusted into his keeping. As he begins to assert his divine rulership he automatically begins his own development and will evolve into the "Life more abundant!"

One lays hold of LIFE, or the power of God, by his own thought actions and his emotional re-actions. Life is vibration! It is pure! Life is ecstatic splendor. It is glorious vibrancy in its fullest expression! Life is love in its highest devotional essence of divine purity! It is hope in all its expectant, reaching power of glorious fulfilment. It is joy in its triumphant splendor of attunement. It is the marvelous song of gratitude expressed in that singing ecstasy of inner praise. It is tenderness and beauty and loveliness and completion—the completion of oneself. It is the fulfilling, triumphant power of eternity.

This divine, glorious gift of LIFE belongs to every man in its fullest abundance as man reaches out and takes hold of It. It is the very Light of Christ made manifest within one's own being as he accepts It and brings It forth. It is the power of God swinging into action from within as one casts out the darkness of his ordinary, mortal thinking habits and takes hold of the gifts and powers of Almighty God.

Life is endless! It is increasing, everlasting glory! It is eternal power! It is joy and happiness and the power of complete fulfilment as one becomes filled with the very "Fulness of God!" This glorious vibration is developed from within. It is established in tenderness and appreciation and joyous gratitude. As the "Life more abundant" is brought forth one progresses into a dynamic, creative individual who becomes the master of his fate as he triumphs over the darkness, the evils and vicissitudes of his life. Then as he continues to fulfill the measure, for which God created him, his life forces expand in ever increasing glory until he reaches the fulfilment of himself in that triumphant transition where he is "changed in the twinkling of an eye from a mortal being into an immortal son of God."

These gifts are yours! They have always been yours. But you must accept them. Remember, "The first requisite to fulfilling is the ability to believe." Then as you live the laws the gifts and powers are your own. None can fulfill the laws for you. None can do your believing for you. None can do your "overcoming" of your doubts and fears and negative thoughts for you. None can receive the great glory for you.

The way is perfect. The plan is unerring and the laws unfailing and divine. You alone have the power to turn "The Battle of Decision" into victory. The choice is your own as you begin to rule over your own dominion—the kingdom of yourself—or relinquish that divine Christhood to the thieves and robbers of the darkness, the usurpers of the Divine Domain— The reward of "overcoming" is not only abundant, beautiful Life but "Life Eternal!"

What is Life eternal? It is the bestowing of all keys and all powers and all good and abundance and joy upon the individual who merits it. It is the stage of existence when nothing can be lost. It is the state in which all perfection is fulfilled and all glory expanded and all joys multiplied. It is the realm in which no sorrow or lack or distress or darkness can possibly exist. It is all that the hungry, yearning soul of man has ever yearned for. It is the full completion of oneself in breathtaking majesty and splendor. Life eternal is the clothing of a man in divinity as love and joy are perfected.

This gift, Christ holds out in everlasting fullness, to those who will only accept His words and fulfill His divine laws of "overcoming". These laws go beyond the creeds and requirements of any earthly church or organization. These are the laws of perfected love, of infinite, tender forgiveness, of established joy and confidence and perfected faith. This is the church and the kingdom of "The First Born". It is the "Brotherhood of Light," or consists of those who have glorified and brought forth the Light as they overcame the darkness of every negative fear and thought and action.

Life Eternal is awaiting every individual on this earth who can only *be-live* and fulfill. It is not something that exists in some far distant, remote, future time. This is awaiting man's acceptance of it NOW. It is yours whenever you prove yourself worthy of Its powers.

THE POWER OF GOD IN ACTION

Chapter XVI

As you marvel over these higher truths, questioning within yourself the possibility of them being fulfilled in you, turn to the true Witness and ask that It reveal the actuality of these things fully to your soul. As you do this humbly and sincerely the "Holy Spirit of Promise" will bear witness to your intellect concerning the truth and the power of this work so that you need never doubt.

Whenever questions of doubt arise, seeking to undermine your hope of fulfilment, turn anew to that "Holy Spirit of Promise" and accept Its unfailing testimony. As you do this Its voice of promise and power will increase within you until all will be made clear and so be fulfilled in you. This "Holy Spirit of Promise" truly "promises all things—and *fulfills* all things!" This "Holy Spirit of Promise" is the very voice of God as it bears witness, through that glorified Light of Christ within, that every divine promise can be fulfilled in YOU.

That "Holy Spirit of Promise" is God's voice of *faith* echoing its unfailing, pledged assurance into your own open heart. As you listen to Its voice you will receive the hope-filled promise of full accomplishment. The gifts are already yours. But you must lay claim to them. As you *be* and *live* according to the vibrant Life force within you, you will receive the *fulness of LIFE*—or the *"Fulness of the Father!"* Then it will be that all things will be fulfilled in you.

As one learns to cast out the doubts and the darkness and the fears, that seek ever to thwart his progress, he will find he is truly *"exercising the great and mighty faith,"* enjoined by the scriptures.

This "exercising of faith" is no more or less than using one's power to *believe* as he eliminates doubting and darkness and negation from his mind under the guidance and power of that "Holy Spirit of Promise," yielding himself fully to Its virtue of completion and fulfilment.

Such are your gifts and powers. And such is God's "Holy Spirit of Promise" inviting you to partake of all the unutterable promises of Life and Eternity—that all might be fulfilled in you.

God bless and sustain you until you have proved these things in your own divine fulfilment. Yes. "Prove all things" is God's urgent request to all men. And *God's laws can only be proved by the living of them.* "Live the laws and you will KNOW of their truth." And the reward and the power will be your own forever and forever!

To KNOW the truth one must LIVE it! One may know *about* truth even as he knows *about* God. But to actually *know* truth or *know* God, one must go beyond the initial, kindergarten stage of belief into the pathway of fulfilment. One must step out beyond the voice of "hear-say" held forth by mortal teachers as they display their feeble "arm of flesh" in their powerless, unfulfilled ideas and precepts.

The Path Christ trod is the path of complete fulfilment for everyone who will travel it. It is the Way which He IS. This is the *Way of Life.* It is the Way which is your own, eternally lighted by the glory of the Savior of men as you follow Him in triumphant, victorious overcoming.

Rejoice evermore! Rejoice as you clothe yourself in Light Eternal! Even the Life more abundant!

Every note of ecstasy, every glimmer of hope, every thought of joy, every song of praise and gratitude are the powers of His Light being released from within your own being. As you keep that song of gratitude and thanks vibrating forth from within you will become glorious. This is the *law*. It cannot fail.

The darkness can be overcome by that vibrating song of thanksgiving originating in your own mind and heart as you send it forth on the wings of your loving appreciation. You hold the key! And you are the door! And yours is the power of the fulfilment of every divine promise ever given unto the children of men.

Begin consciously to express Life in joyous gratitude for every gift and blessing, no matter how seemingly insignificant, and Life will flow to you in ever increasing abundance until "you overcome the evils of your life and lose every desire for sin and are wrapped in the power and glory of your Maker and are caught up to dwell with Him."

If one considers for but a moment the effort and the time required to gather up the treasures of earth, that are subject to thieves and moths and termites and rust and decay and destruction, and begins to share just a portion of that time and energy to fulfill the things of the Spirit he will begin to grow into the powers of eternity.

This time and energy used in fulfilling the higher laws of God has been mistakenly spent, if one assumes he is righteous, in trying to convert others to his own way of thinking. Christianity has fought and squabbled and failed because of this erroneous idea. Any individual who will use his strength in perfecting himself, as he learns to travel that sacred, inner Way of "overcoming," will draw others to him. He will not need to go out to find them. Neither will he need to seek to hold their minds by the force of his wordy haranguements. They, "seeing his Light" will come to him as they glorify God by seeking to bring that same Light forth within themselves. As this Light becomes manifest within any individual it brings forth an automatic "chain reaction" for others will seek for the fulfilling power of Its glory.

As one learns to perfect himself, instead of trying painfully to perfect everyone else, he will grow into the unspeakable powers of heaven naturally, beautifully and gloriously.

"The Great Brotherhood of Light," even the members of the "Church of the Firstborn" are awaiting those who bring forth Christ's holy Light within themselves. To such is given the "Life more abundant!" And that "Life more abundant" is but the beginning of the "Life which is Eternal!" The "Life Eternal" follows the "Life more abundant" as naturally as maturity follows youth, as summer follows spring or as the harvest follows the planting. Each is the full completion of the other.

"Nothing is impossible to him who believes." He who believes will *be* and *live* according to the precepts his open heart accepts and his enlightened mind comprehends.

In following belief one steps into the power of *faith!* Faith goes beyond belief. As one *lives* the higher laws the "Holy Spirit of Promise" begins to make all things more clear. The soul of man is thus quickened and the principle of *faith* develops until that inner "seat of knowing" begins to voice the eternal truths of God and one steps beyond the boundaries of mortal established facts and procedures.

Faith however must be exercised in order to develop into power. An infant must develop its lungs and muscles through activity in order to grow. A youth must develop his mind through schooling, and an adult his skills and talents through performance. But all who would reach that point of power must "exercise great and mighty faith" simply by keeping the doubts and fears out.

"And Christ truly said unto our Fathers, if ye have faith ye can do all things which are expedient unto me.

"And now I speak unto all the ends of the earth—that if the day cometh that the power and gifts of God shall be done away among you, it shall be because of unbelief.

"And woe be unto the children of men if this be the case, for there shall be none that doeth good among you, no, not one. For if there be one among you that doeth good, he shall work by the power and gifts of God.

"And woe unto them who shall do these things away and die, for *they shall die in their sins,* and they cannot be saved in the kingdom of God; and I speak it according to the words of Christ; and I lie not."

What has become of the gifts and the powers of God and the faith that brought them forth?

"For who shall say that Jesus Christ did not do many mighty miracles? And there were mighty miracles wrought by the hands of his apostles.

"And if there were miracles wrought then, why has God ceased to be a God of miracles and yet be an unchangeable Being? And behold I say unto you he changeth not;

if so he would cease to be God; and he ceaseth not to be God, and is a God of miracles.

"And the reason why he ceaseth to do miracles among the children of men is because that they dwindled in unbelief, and depart from the right WAY, and know not the God in whom they should trust.

"Behold, I say unto you that whoso believeth in Christ, DOUBTING NOTHING, whatsoever he shall ask the Father in the Name of Christ, it shall be granted him; and this promise is unto all, even to the ends of the earth!"

". . . . . And now, my beloved brethren, if this be the case that these things are true which I have spoken unto you, and God will show unto you, with power and great glory at the last day, that they are true, and if they are true has the day of miracles ceased?

"Or have angels ceased to appear unto the children of men? Or has he withheld the power of the Holy Ghost from them? Or will he so long as time shall last, or the earth shall stand, or there shall be one man upon the face thereof to be saved? Behold, I say unto you, Nay; for it is by faith that miracles are wrought; and it is by faith that angels appear and minister unto men; wherefore, if these things have ceased woe be unto the children of men, for it is because of unbelief, AND ALL IS VAIN."

Now to explain what *faith* is and how it works.

Thoughts, or desires, or hopes form the pattern or mold that faith or the spiritual substance or material of creative power must fill. The mold must be filled even as a bucket is filled with water when it is dipped into the sea. The water is literally drawn into the container. It has no other course but to enter and fill full—or fulfill the open vessel.

As this divine substance is drawn into the form, or pattern of one's ardent hopes, and held until it is congealed or completely established it becomes tangible to the physical senses of man. In other words, "as one goes into his secret closet to hold communion with God he will be rewarded openly." The very desires he holds within his heart will become manifest in concrete, tangible form. They become realities.

Faith, in action, is an ordinance of functioning that reaches beyond mortal senses and physical laws to fulfill whatsoever man can lift his spiritual eyes or vision to behold or desire.

Whatsoever one "hopes for" must be fulfilled unless man's own perverse thinking destroys the pattern by his entertained fears and doubts. Doubts and fears are punc- sacred fluid of creation escapes. This creative substance is tures in the bucket or mold and through these holes the *faith*.

"And Jesus said unto them, Because of your unbelief; for verily I say unto you, if ye have faith as a grain of mustard seed, ye shall say unto this mountain, Remove hence to yonder place; and it shall remove; and nothing shall be impossible unto you." (Matt. 17:20) Or as it is given in Mark 11:23: "For verily I say unto you, That whosoever shall say unto this mountain, Be thou removed, and be thou cast into the sea; and *shall not doubt in his heart, but shall believe that those things which he saith shall come to pass: He shall have whatsoever he saith. Wherefore I say unto you, What things soever ye desire when ye pray, believe that ye receive them and ye shall have them.*"

"If one has FAITH as *a grain of mustard seed*" all things become possible unto him.

A mustard seed is a living thing that will grow without

attention or care. The life force exists within it. It only needs to be planted. *The seed of faith,* like the mustard seed needs only to be established and left to grow. A seed's very nature endows it with the power to draw to itself all that is required to fulfill the pattern or plan of its own being. The only things that can destroy or uproot it after it is planted are the fears and doubts and negative attitudes of man's own mortal, contrary thinking.

Faith is truly a living seed that can gather to itself the fulness of anything man can imagine. Faith is a substance that is alive. It is an essence, a material, a divine element that will gather to itself all that is required to fulfill the idea, the plan or the pattern or the hope held forth for its fulfilling.

Faith is a power. It is not a dead *belief* or a mortal reliance upon some creed or doctrine. Faith is a living *power.* It definitely is a substance of unutterable potency. It carries with it the full potentiality of all that it embraces, even the complete fulfilling to bring forth any ideal or plan held forth by man's true thinking.

Faith is always man's to use. It holds within it joy and fulfilment and glorious completion. It is the power of creation. It is the building material of Gods—and men. Even the worlds were created by Faith, or of Faith. Man himself was made out of its ethereal substance gathered into his own material form.

God's holy edict or command, "LET THERE BE—" is the expression of His own divine plan held forth to be filled with that creative essence or "substance of things hoped for."

"Behold, when ye shall rend the veil of unbelief which doth cause you to remain in your awful state of wickedness, and hardness of heart, and blindness of mind, then shall the great and marvelous things that have been hid up from the foundation of the world from you begin to be made manifest through your own fulfilling.

Hold to the "hope of your desires, without doubting in your heart" and the law is that your hopes must be fulfilled. This law is irrevocable and eternal. It cannot fail. This is faith in action. "And according to your faith it will be done unto you." Your own degree of faith will be according to your own activity of mind and heart in exercising it.

Remember, you are the container for the mold or pattern into which the creative substance of fulfilment must flow. If you are filled with doubts and fears the pattern or mold is made useless and of no worth. It becomes an open sieve through which the divine essence is lost and wasted.

Your degree of faith will be according to your own activity of mind and heart in exercising it.

Faith is a spiritual substance. It is an essence, shall we say, because of its intangibility to mortal senses. Nevertheless it is a completing ingredient of unutterable power which all men can use who desire to accomplish anything. It must be used also by those who bring to pass the fulfilling of their own destiny in its completed glory.

"Without faith it is impossible to please God." Only negation, doubts and fears and dismays and man's own evils can possibly keep faith from fulfilling and perfecting all things. Therefore God cannot possibly be pleased with those who have no degree of faith. Theirs' is only the power to destroy, not fulfill. Faith is the spiritual substance, the divine element that must be used if man is to

fulfill the measure of his own creation and accomplish anything of lasting good.

As one lives the laws of the kingdom he is interested
in, or concerns himself with, he becomes a member of that
kingdom. If he lives the higher laws then he must advance
into the higher kingdom where *faith* becomes the substance of fulfilment. Faith is by far a greater force or
power than electricity. It is the essence or material as well
as the compelling force out of which all things are formed.
"Faith is the substance of things hoped for!" It is the material out of which they are created and established and
completed. Instead of splitting atoms and dispersing them
in adverse, contrary, fantastic explosions of destruction,
faith gathers these same spiritual atoms into form to fill
the mold or the pattern his mind holds forth.

Indeed, "Faith promises all things and fulfills all things!"
"The Holy Spirit of Promise" and the principle or element
of Faith are inseparable. One holds forth the pattern the
other will fulfill.

It must also be understood that faith is only beautiful
and of lasting value when it is allied with love. It is quite
possible to use a degree of faith without the gift of love
being present. But without love faith is a cold, bleak, soulless process of inglorious selfishness.

"For though I speak with the tongues of men and of
angels, and have not love, I am become as sounding brass
or a clanging cymbal.

"And though I have the gift of prophecy, and understand all mysteries, and all knowledge; and though I have
all faith, so that I could remove mountains, and have not
love, I am nothing.

"And though I bestow all my goods to feed the poor,

and though I give my body to be burned, and have not love, it profiteth me nothing."

Only as this precious gift of faith is aligned with love can it become glorious and eternal. Use the powers of faith. But use them with love and your Light shall so shine that others seeing your good works will glorify God forever.

Beloved, *Be Come* all that you can possibly imagine or hope for. The Way is now your own! Come! Step into the "Life more abundant!" It has been promised to you from the very beginning. Only your own doubts and fears and ignorance, as you have permitted the traditions of your fathers to defile you, have kept it from you. As this abundant Life becomes your own you will have the power to take the next step—the step into that divine "Eternal Life!" "All that the Father has is yours!"

Leave the inglorious way of death for those who worship the road their ancestors and predecessors have trod—the way of the flesh.

When the majority first read these books they wait expectantly for someone to come along who will lift them into the great perfection. Others wait idly inactive expecting God to do it for them. Most seem to lack the initiative to face the fact that they must throw aside their apathy and make that great transition for God—not God for them.

This great step into the higher spiritual realm must be taken by man. As one exerts himself to take hold of the higher laws and fulfills them he begins to achieve the "impossible," for that which appeared to be "impossible" becomes *"possible."* Yes. "All things *are possible* to him who believes!" As one begins to live the higher laws he most assuredly proves them. In doing so his belief grows

into faith and faith becomes power as it fulfills, or fills
full, the pattern of his own perfect design and his own hopes.

There is no mystery about the principle of faith and the
law upon which it works. It is as exact and as perfect and
unfailing as any chemical law in the laboratory of the most
exacting science. Anyone who desires can prove it. He
needs only to exert himself to begin the experiment and
then to follow it through. In so doing he requires no expensive equipment for he himself is the sacred crucible.

There is one more thing that must be placed in this
record before it is sealed and sent forth to encompass the
earth.

The key of complete mastery and divine accomplishment
is a simple task that unfolds out of the ordinary, as well
as the intense, moments of living.

This is truly "a lone and dreary world" because the vibrations arising from it are so filled with despair, anguish,
suffering, greed, jealousies, defiance and rebellion, they are
overwhelming in their intensity. When one is relaxed and
unaware of their bombarding impact of detrimental fury,
these destructive vibrations usually make their attacks. These
devastating vibrations of negation and evil seize upon the
individual in full force whenever an opportunity arises in
which to shatter his peace of mind and bring havoc into
his life. However, the most dismal vibrations of dismay
can never touch the man who keeps his own vibrations high
in a song of inner glory that arises in joyous ecstacies of
living love and gratitude out of the devotion of his own
heart. It is only when one's own vibrations are lowered
that the darkness and dismays can enter. And it is always
in those moments of darkness that one's misfortunes are
born and released. The disasters and calamities can never

touch the man who is aware of Christ's great Light contained within himself. Man always has the power to consciously hold himself within Its glow. As he abides in that vibration of living Light, It truly abides in him. This is "the armor of Christ" which the Saints are counseled to clothe themselves in.

This is a "lone and dreary world" because it is so completely enfolded in the destructive, disastrous vibrations of darkness. They are always seething and struggling to gain access to one's mind and heart—and life. And it is always when these strident powers of evil gain control that one's disasters and misfortunes are bred and hurled into existence.

In those violent moments, or hours of dismay and desolation, one has but to call upon that inner Light, as he sends forth that silent prayer of love and thanks and glory to disperse the darkness and all that it contains. With such a released vibration of loving prayer, the seeming disasters or evils dissolve into nothingness, as they return to the shadows from which they come forth. They have no power to withstand the living rays of that magnified Christ Light as it is released through a man's own open soul.

It is most assuredly true that "All things work together for good to them that love the Lord."

Whatever dismal, overwhelming condition may appear to exist, it can be transmuted into a blessing as soon as one stands up in his divine right to exercise his mastery over his own thoughts and vibrations regarding that adversity. As one becomes the Master of his own thoughts and vibrations, he becomes the master of the conditions that come into his life by aligning himself with God. Then it is that "The Father within can do the works" of perfecting all conditions and all things, as He brings to pass the things of heaven on the earthly plane.

At first the individual will not have the power to choose what every condition in his life will be, but as he struggles against the darkness, for mastery over himself, the outcome of those conditions will be transformed into good. One may not be able to control every happening immediately but, as he exerts himself to bring forth only the glory of Christ's Light, in a prayer of love and gratitude and gracious obedience, the results of those happenings will become the shining wonder of his own existence. All evils will be transmuted into blessings as the Father is permitted to accomplish His works of glory, through man.

Soon the results of such control in thoughts and vibrations become so powerful, only the most beautiful things can possibly happen in that individual's life. As the individual exerts his power of control over himself he becomes the master. And that mastery expands to include conditions and things and the man's entire life. His hands become filled with blessings and goodness and infinite love. Then it is, he permits "the Father within" to express His perfection as His Kingdom and power of Heaven is brought forth in the material world.

He who develops the ability to control those anguished moments of dismay and those dismal tumultuous periods of disaster, as he brings forth that inner vibration of living Light released through peace and prayer, will soon be lifted high in consciousness so that he will have the power to "overcome all the evils of his life." As this Light is magnified and increased within one, he will soon be prepared to behold the face of God, which has been promised from the beginning.

To behold the face of God is the eternal, living invitation to every man. Yes, "seek me diligently and ye shal' find me!" Or accept the promise as it stands forth in these words: "This is life eternal, to know Thee, the only true and living God; and Jesus Christ whom He has sent."

Hold your vibrations in loving, tender confidence and peace, as you worship and adore in every seeming calamity and every dire distress, and watch those evils melt away.

Hold your vibrations in love and kindness when hate and discords are hurled at you by another and behold the daggers of his wrath fall impotently at your feet, as you gather up the Light, multiplied and increased.

These are the keys of Mastery and of glory and Eternal Life. They are yours to use. They have always been yours.

Live these higher laws of love and gratitude and power and you will know of their truth—"And the truth will make you free!"

"The Spirit and the bride say, Come! And let him that heareth say, Come! And let him that is athirst come! And whosoever will, let him take of the waters of life *freely!*"

So have I been commanded to write. And so it is written—Amen!

THE CELESTIAL SONG OF CREATION

By Annalee Skarin

APPENDIX

APPENDIX

The gift or principle of faith is to be used to accomplish the impossible. The things that are humanly possible do not require the dynamic "exercising of great and mighty faith."

Great and mighty faith demands a great and mighty project or goal or undertaking. It demands what orthodoxed, mortal minds consider to be impossible.

As one lifts his vision to the glory of God his vision expands to comprehend the greater goals. As his understanding is exalted his desires become purified and spiritualized until nothing appears to be impossible.

So it is, that when one fully comprehends the purpose and the power of faith all things become possible. Faith is truly the substance out of which things "hoped for" are formed or created. Faith is more. It is the principle of creation in action. "Faith promises all things for it is allied with the Holy Spirit of Promise. And it fulfills all things," as one learns to exercise it.

Faith, like love, never fails. It is man who fails to use a privilege and a power so great. It is easier to drift along in the deep maze of human taboos and creeds, than to rise up above one's doubts and fears and mediocre existence, to exert the divine powers of creation and fulfilment. This is simply because man has never truly believed the unspeakable, stupendous promises of Almighty God.

Man adheres to some creed or doctrine or church and misthinks he is exercising faith. All he is really doing is weakly shifting the responsibility of his eternal welfare, as well as his moral obligations, onto the shoulders of the orthodoxed leaders of his choice. This adherence to "the arm of flesh" is not faith. It is slothfulness. It could even be called stupidity. At best, one is cheating his soul, as he remains "a blind follower of the blind" in his physical distresses, human miseries and powerless beliefs.

As one holds his desire or hope, without wavering or changing or doubting, in a diligent effort to maintain a conscious awareness of the desire at all times, he is exercising faith. The more intense the desire, the more intense will become the effort, until one is automatically exercising great and mighty faith. Faith is a stupendous, active power of creative force that must fulfill the hope or ideal or desire, which is held forth for its fulfilling. Faith has no other course than to fulfill itself, as it draws into the container, or pattern, of the desire, the substance of creation to bring forth in tangible form, the hope held out.

For Columbus it took eighteen years. The ignorance and fears of centuries had to be overcome. Yet the dream of the youth became the establish facts of a world.

Faith is the foundation or law of fulfilment. It is the principle of achievement. It is the power of complete accomplishment. It is the gift of creation, of restoration, of renewal and of perfection as well as exaltation. To faith "nothing is impossible." It can fulfill the seemingly impossible as readily as a man's slightest wish. Only faith can reach out to take hold of all the powers of the universe and deliver them fulfilled into man's hands—or into his life.

Faith is every man's to use. None have a monopoly upon it. It is a principle or law of such dynamic, stupendous creative power, all things are possible and of easy accomplishment, as one opens his mind to comprehend and to exercise the precious *gift* of creation. And none can exercise it without benefiting a world.

A dull, stupid, inactive belief is not faith. Faith is *power in ACTION!* It is the principle of creation as it is put into use.

It will take patience, at first, to fulfill the deepest desires of one's soul, because the exercising of great and mighty faith may demand that one perfect himself, as well as the container or idea or ideal he holds out to be fulfilled—or filled full of the creative substance of God. Or as James so aptly stated: "Let patience have her perfect work that ye might be perfect and entire, wanting nothing!" The idea, or desire, or goal, must be held forth in perfect, unwavering clarity until the very mold takes on the faultless perfection that admits no doubts or fears or inherent human ideas to mar it.

This is how faith works, as its impossible achievements are consummated in purest perfection. This is how every hope can be fulfilled and every desire be accomplished.

To use faith in this manner, one must be sure he is not working selfishly, in contrary willfulness to the divine Will of God. In God's Will, all perfection, all beauty, all loveliness, exists for the present and for the future. Any evil, selfish desire can bring no glory with it. And to use the gift of faith to interfere with another's free-agency is disastrous.

As one purifies his hopes and desires to reach into the

higher realms, they become as perfect as the principle of fulfilment.

Reach beyond all *possible* things into the dynamic achievements of unutterable power and glory as you use the divine gift of faith to bring forth your heaven on earth, to glorify God and to fulfill the promises of Jesus Christ, the Savior of the world.

Hold forth the withered arm, the crippled limbs or the unseeing eyes and let patience and faith have their perfect work.

When you have perfected yourself in the use of faith, time is no longer required in the fulfilling process. Hold forth the five loaves and the three small fishes and have them instantly multiplied into an over-abundance. In the power of faith, is contained the supply for all your needs and for all the necessities of your life, for these things will all be added unto you as you "seek for the Kingdom of God to fulfill its righteousness," or to use its principles rightly. When you perfect the use of the law its action becomes instantaneous.

Go beyond human thought or belief or orthodoxed, conformed ideas of dead, dogmatic acceptance. "Doubt not! Fear not!" The principle and the power of faith is yours to use at all times. Exercise it! Use it! Perfect it! And you yourself will grow perfect in its use for nothing will remain impossible to you.

Look not at the distresses and the lacks. Concentrate on what you do possess and bless and give thanks. If you, or mayhap your loved one, has only a broken, marred body in which the feeble pulse of life throbs weakly, hold out that gift of life within the perfect mold of your conscious, loving heart and bless and give thanks as you praise and rejoice and that feeble flicker of life will be increased to its fullest measure, according to the perfection of your own idea. Remember your idea or hope-filled awareness is the container or mold which gathers into itself the substance of creation and of fulfilment.

With the correct use of this creative principle, your lacks can and will be supplied, as your life is made perfect and powerful with the impelling principle of faith exercised to fulfill the "impossible!" "Yea, all that the Father has is yours." Use it!

Nothing is too great to desire—that is righteous. Nothing is too prodigious to accomplish and nothing is impossible when the marvelous, creative power of faith is brought into action by your own correct thinking processes as you hold your idea or ideal or request forth to Its limitless, fulfilling measure of creation. Let your minds reach out to encompass and contemplate the promises that have been given—promises to fulfill all that Christ fulfilled—and more! Hold to those promises, in faith, that they might be fulfilled for the eternal glory of God—and your own also.

Truly, "Nothing is impossible to him who believes!"

"Faith is the substance of things hoped for, the EVI-DENCE of things not seen." Things that are seen do not require faith. Faith is the "evidence" or the indicator of facts that are not visible. It is the dynamic road along which proof is uncovered and established.

The first shred of *evidence* in any investigation may be only a thread, a hair, a grain of sand misplaced. It may seem to be too insignificant and infinitesimal to demand that a search be made along its suggested indications. It may take imaginative fortitude and slowly accumulating confidence, to follow that trail through to its surprising end, as it reveals the unseen facts with indisputable certainty.

Faith truly contains the power to "PROVE ALL THINGS!"

Every man is a living record of unquestionable *evidence*, which, if explored, will unveil the stupendous realities of that which, at first, was unapparent and unseen.

Man carries within himself the *evidence* that he is much more than a mere physical being of flesh and blood and bones. Man has a mind with which to think and reason and investigate—and choose. He has a heart with which to love in self-sacrificing tenderness and with which to adore in sublime devotion as he kneels at the very throne of God in worshipping homage of singing glory. He has a soul that can reach and yearn and aspire and KNOW—and fulfill. Yet none of these facts can be seen with human eyes. This very unseen evidence is enough to set a man upon a search of eternal truth and power if he will only open up the inner realm of his thinking capacity to contemplate and weigh the *evidence* his physical eyes has never looked upon. To accomplish this it may be necessary to open up the mind and remove the seals of blindness that have been established by a life-time of thinking or even generations of dogmatic errors.

"Faith is truly the *evidence* of things unseen." *Evidence* is the indicators, or guide-posts or way-marks along the upward path into the higher realms. This *evidence*, which is faith, contains the proof which can reveal the definite reality behind the promises of God—and to fulfill them.

Faith has been called *"blind"* by the mocking, unbelievers in belittling contempt. No statement could be more false. Faith is never blind. Faith is endowed with a deeper, truer, *knowing* vision. What is called "blind faith" is only some unprogressive, mortal concept or acceptance of a dead creed or belief. This is not faith! Faith is always active and alive. It is continually revealing and fulfilling the greater possibilities a searching mind holds out in earnest contemplation in its quest of *knowing*. Faith cannot possibly be blind. Neither can it be inactive. Only dull indifference or stupid unbelief are blind. And only sealed, orthodoxed minds remain inactive in a smug, unholy, complacent contentment that leads to death.

Faith contains the *evidence* that will prove and fulfill every promise, every hope and every worthy desire as one seeks to follow that *evidence* through to its source.

There is much, much more that could be said upon *faith as an evidence* of things which are not seen but I am restrained from revealing the entire pattern of its wonders.

Let me suggest only that *evidence* must be checked and proved else it is of no value. There is no limit to faith's supply of continually increasing evidence as one follows its leading. And that *evidence* will grow into definite, eternal knowledge as one puts it to use. As faith is exercised the unseen becomes visible and will be established in tangible, indisputable reality. So is the law of creation fulfilled. And so does "Faith promise all things—and fulfills all things!" To faith nothing is impossible!

Faith reveals the evidence of "the substance of those things hoped for." And as one uses that substance of creation new *evidence* is continually produced to substantiate every claim and to fulfill every promise as the gates of glory finally open wide to welcome the searching traveler home in honor.

"Ask, seek and knock, for everyone who asks receives

and he who seeks finds, and to him who knocks it shall be opened," even the doors to all truth and to all power.

———————

This work has been given that man might rend the veil of darkness that enshrouds the earth and the powers of God in the unholy condition of the great wickedness of unbelief.

This work contains the keys by which one might "PROVE ALL THINGS as he learns to hold fast to that which is good!"

The promises Christ left with the world have become buried in fear and superstition and doubting as the dark mist of the ages has accumulated to enfold His miraculous powers in awesome whispers of fearsome mystery. By the slothful ones and the cowards, who are afraid to face truth and take hold of Its Light, the seals of ignorance and darkness have been perpetuated and increased upon the earth. And by these sealed and unenlightened ones who have only professed to believe, but who have never lived the laws, faith has been denied, truth has been silenced and light has been banished. Sealed hearts and closed, blinded minds are the encompassing, confining walls of hell as a man permits himself to be locked in by his own accepted unprogressiveness and encouraged unbelief. And by such, doubts and fears have been engendered and fostered upon the whole human race.

"And Christ truly said unto our fathers, if ye have faith ye can do all things which are expedient unto me." To do *"the things that are expedient"* means to be able to use the power of God to glorify every condition as it arises, to heal those one meets along his way and to bless each happening by enfolding it in the power and love of the Lord as faith is permitted to do her perfect work. The dismal, mortal happenings one faces in life, the distresses of the world, the sorrows and afflictions of one's fellowmen, these are the "expedient" needs Christ is speaking of. And these expedient circumstances will be yours to meet and to overcome by the power and Light of Jesus Christ, Son of the Living God as you begin to use the divine principle of faith.

Now, to continue with the quotation: "And now I speak unto all the ends of the earth—that if the day cometh that the power and gifts of God shall be done away among you, it shall be because of unbelief.

"And woe be unto the children of men if this be the case, for there shall be none that doeth good among you, NO NOT *ONE!*" For *if there be ONE among you that doeth good, he shall work by the power and gifts of God.*

"And woe unto them who shall do these things away and die, for *they shall die in their sins,* and they cannot be saved in the kingdom of God; and I speak it according to the words of Christ; and I lie not!"

In our day and age mahkind has almost succeeded in "doing away with the powers and gifts of God" by mocking derision and unbelieving skepticism. Many have designated God's divine gifts as "evil" and those who believe in them are regarded as deceivers and heretics to be shunned and avoided. Or else they are branded as fanatics, devoid of intelligence. Those who have denied these powers to others have lost them completely themselves—and realize it not.

While those who may still have hunches that defy explanation and reach beyond the realm of doubt, have only courage enough to mention them in timid whispers to some sympathetic friend they trust will not betray them and their sacred confidence.

Who is there in this day and age with the courage to stand up and declare with Paul in the powerful assertion of confident assurance: *"I believe all things! I hope all things!"* and understand that *faith* IS the substance of those things *hoped* for as it is gathered into form to fulfill the unwavering, undoubting hope or idea?

For such this work has come forth by the power and grace of God that all who will might become purified by living the higher laws and by casting aside the veil of unbelief in the exercising of a great and mighty faith that will fulfill all things. "For the veil will soon be rent and he who is not purified shall not abide the day!"

So has God spoken! And so have I been commanded to write by the power of the Almighty God, Creator of heaven and of earth!

And in the Name of Jesus Christ this record is sealed up unto the righteous forever for the wicked will never be able to lay hold of it nor fulfill its promises.

And who are the righteous?

The righteous are those who are not so lost in sin or so secured by pride and wickedness and self-righteousness and orthodoxed opinions they cannot humble themselves in prayer to ask God, in the Name of His Beloved Son, Jesus Christ, whether these things are true or not.

The righteous are the ones who love the truth and continue to search for it along that divine highway of increasing *evidence* which faith unfolds. They are the ones with the spiritual courage to live by the truth when they find it. These are God's noble ones who are not burdened with the ponderous weights of self-righteousness, self-pity or who are blinded by willfully sealed minds. To those who are sealed in unprogressive darkness the container or mold, in which the sublime substance of creation is gathered, is inverted and holds no promise or power of fulfillment.

Every living soul who will ask sincerely to know the truth of these things will have the truth of them revealed by the power of the Holy Ghost. "And by the power of the Holy Ghost they may *know the truth* of all things!"

So is the law of the Lord. And so is His power of fulfilment. And so have I been ordained to testify and commanded to write that these truths might be sealed up unto the righteous forever.

And so have I written according to the command given unto me—In the Name of the Father and of the Son and of the Holy Ghost—Amen!

CPSIA information can be obtained
at www.ICGtesting.com
Printed in the USA
BVHW081625010619
549889BV00003B/120/P